OASIS

What's the Story?

OASIS

What's the Story?

IAIN ROBERTSON

mp
MUSIC
PRESS

Published by Music Press Books
an imprint of John Blake Publishing Ltd
3 Bramber Court, 2 Bramber Road,
London W14 9PB, England

www.johnblakebooks.co.uk

www.facebook.com/johnblakebooks 🇫
twitter.com/jblakebooks 🇪

First published in paperback in 1996
This edition published in 2016

ISBN: 978 1 78606 038 9

British Library Cataloguing-in-Publication Data:

A catalogue record for this book is available from the British Library.

Design by www.envydesign.co.uk

Printed in Great Britain by CPI

1 3 5 7 9 10 8 6 4 2

Papers used by John Blake Publishing are natural, recyclable products made from
wood grown in sustainable forests. The manufacturing processes conform to the
environmental regulations of the country of origin.

Dedicated to impossible things:
God knows why
and for Mum,
and for Mums,
and for Mams.

Thanks
to Jake
for criticism,
for enthusiasm,
for ideas.

To Andrew Eldritch
for allowing me the words to 'Floorshow'...

To Ian Hunter
for Diary of a Rock and Roll Star...

and

To Stiletto:
for Rapier Wit, and Taking no Shit

CONTENTS

FOREWORD

REMARKABLY, IT HAS BEEN SOME twenty years since this story was first told and a whole shitload of toxic water has passed under a number of burning bridges since then - but the facts remain. Oasis did it right. Xylophones, clowns, balloons, 2D wannabes and other bullshit bubblegum ephemera: not in evidence. Analogue rock & roll, made for an irreverent generation, fuelled with marching powder, premium lager and an unswerving commitment to hitting the 'fun' button.

No compromise.

No prisoners.

Ever.

Fortunately, I was there. Or perhaps I wasn't. Really can't be entirely certain. You see, there were multiple theatres of operation; everything louder than everything else – and sometimes it was hard to tell. Of course, I was at the epicentre: but these were strange days, and there was plenty of notable crazy on the edges. Unless I missed something though, this is a reasonable account of un-reasonable things.

Wild times, then.

I wish, for me, it hadn't had to stop.

That said – it took its toll.

Hard to figure how different life would be if one had zigged instead of zagged. Leaving any sentimentality to one side, you are left with the old adage: 'If the horse hadn't stopped for a piss, it would have won the race'. Officially, the band were not thrilled that I shared any of the contents herein – in fact, having bumped into most of them, on a number of occasions since publishing, they were all pretty relaxed about it.

Validation? Not really, and not needed.

Evidence, rather, that this is how it was; Noel, when I met him, at one or other NME awards event, observed kindly that *What's the Story* is 'the best account of MY band – and the truth'– that'll do for me.

Conventional wisdom suggests that a re-union is inevitable, that there must be one last roll of crooked dice, another messy interaction with a world left wanting more.

Oasis, of course, have always thrown two fingers up at con-vention.

Never say never? Yeah, maybe – but since splitting, the two key players have been thrown into very different and contrasting dramatic trajectory.

Simply put: Noel has gone from strength to strength, while Liam seems a little less certain of the world: although phenomenally successful with his 'Pretty Green' empire, musically it's been a markedly splintered story.

That is what it is.

Anyway, as rumours intensify around whether or not some iteration of the many-headed monster will re-emerge, blinking into the spotlight, armed to the teeth and ready, once more, to unleash hell, I hope the stories and memories shared within these pages will shed a little light on how it all began.

Nothing is certain but the past.

The future is not ours to see, and some things never change – until they do, pass the crystal, spread the tarot, cross everything and throw up a prayer to whichever dishevelled gods are listening for one final hurrah: they were the last great rock 'n' roll band, and the louder we screamed, the faster they went.

And in the end the love you take is equal to the love you make.
'The End' — Lennon and McCartney

CHAPTER 1

THE END

The artist has also an introverted disposition and has not far to go to become neurotic. He is one who is urged on by his instinctual needs which are too clamorous...
SIGMUND FREUD

LIFE ON THE ROAD is obviously not the same as working in a bank, a shop, a garage or anything, in fact, that might be said to give you a proper job. Life and work inside the cocoons that protect society's idols and icons is other than this: life at the centre of the Oasis phenomenon that bleeds across the planet is other than other than this.

Even so, I knew I wasn't having an ordinary day when Liam landed a jarring blow to the side of my head in the middle of a Parisian boulevard as traffic careered around us left and right. There had been earlier clues: his throwing himself from the record company Mercedes as it raced through the same boulevards – a definite sign that all was less than normal, even in such an abnormal world. On the other hand, casting furniture around a restaurant in protest at having to share radio time with the highly talented cross-dressing comedian Eddie Izzard – well, that was typical. I can forgive myself for not seeing then how my day was shaking out. Had I been the seventh son of a seventh son, my psychic antennae would have been hissing like a rattlesnake's arse when, not ten minutes after checking in, the French riot police taped off our hotel after a terrorist bomb threat. No bomb was found, but a Mancunian incendiary device was there, sure enough, informing the French press of his omnipotence, lashing back vodka and orange and ticking like a motherfucker. Liam Gallagher was primed to blow.

Ask Noel, Bonehead, Guigsy or Alan where Liam is and you will inevitably be asked, 'Which one?' In fact, ask anyone who really knows him and they'll tell you that, at any given time, there is a multitude of different personalities fighting for space behind the expressionless eyes. God only knows how he lives in that head – I couldn't. Unfortunately for me, in the role I played as road manager, minder and all things filed under miscellaneous, getting into Liam's head and channelling the poison was part of the job and was, unquestionably, the hardest part. How could I process his chaos in order to enable him to interface with an unsuspecting world?

It was September 1995 and we were in Paris to fulfil an important, but fairly leisurely, press and promotion commitment. Present: band members Liam, Guigsy and Alan; myself from the Oasis inner circle; Linda Gibson from the record company. Linda brought willowy good looks and a corporate credit card; both had become pliable and essential features of these trips abroad. At this point, I figured the plastic was more flexible. Not my first mistake, but a big one.

* * *

Today is a good day – God knows it's certainly better than packing underpants into boxes in Scunthorpe. We settle back in a first-class carriage on the Eurostar, worrying about whether champagne or Chablis would be more appropriate with the grilled salmon. It is out of the question that a chain of events has begun that will lead to a founder member of the band breaking down, and to my own departure from the Oasis camp.

The old town looks the same as we step down from the train and there to meet us is Michel, record-company executive and possessor of yet another credit card to play with. A mercenary attitude? I freely put up my hand. After ten years spent working with bands, I've realised that so much is recoupable and that the musicians are often not as lucky or long-lasting as their crew. However, you can bet on the record companies remaining wealthy. I firmly believe that, when the opportunity presents itself, make the label dig into its pockets: for the artist, this is probably the one ride on the carousel. It's a savage industry and corporate money is seldom anything more than a Trojan horse.

Checking into the hotel involves the familiar ritual of watching the ice maidens on reception (famed for their impassive help) giggle like schoolgirls as the band slouch through the formalities, shades very much on. Oasis, like the Rolling Stones before them, are not the best-looking band in the world but there is a confidence, a street arrogance, bred from their utter conviction that this is their time. Those who come into contact with the band can feel this and it has the strangest effect on all but the most self-composed.

Guigsy follows his luggage to his room; Alan and Liam head straight for the bar; it is five o'clock in the afternoon and already I am the only member of our posse who isn't completely shitfaced.

As the interview treadmill begins, there is no sign of Guigsy. International double-act, Gallagher and White, are unleashing the wit and wisdom that has become their trademark, which is to say that Liam is talking and everyone, Alan included, is listening. The bar on the first floor of the Hotel du Nord is a sight for sore eyes: a spaghetti-western bordello, with a new breed of debauched rock 'n' roller standing in for bad-ass cowboy. Liam and Alan are perfectly at home in their own fancy-dress costumes – ice-cool scally chic. The bartender, with standard coffee and pathos eyes, is doing brisk business, the vodka and orange now being chased down with premium lager. Liam, ever poker-faced, a shoot 'em dead, brain-bell-jangler gambler, wears a double-breasted saffron safari jacket and out-attitudes the bartender. The jacket was bought in Shibuya, Tokyo, a long way from Burnage, Manchester. The bartender's eyes were made long ago from generations of curt Anglo-French relations. But there is no contest: Gallagher wins hands down.

The guys are now on to journalist number three and there is no sign of Guigsy. I decide to check his suite as there is no response to my repeated telephone calls. I find his den and hammer on the door until my knuckles sing. Now it's time to employ the age-old and extremely unpopular pass-key manoeuvre. This involves persuading a chambermaid that the room in question is yours, that you have lost your key and that you desperately need to get in. It's actually far less complicated than a long, rambling tale of an unconscious star needing to be somewhere else other than the land of nod. I find a maid and throw some sentences in garbled French at her only to discover that she speaks embarrassingly good English. She lets me in with a smile and, sure enough, everybody's favourite bass player is spread-eagled, naked across his bed, fast asleep. The maid hovers at the door, blushing, but makes no attempt to leave. I don't have time to worry about her impression of this scene and wake Guigsy with some difficulty to remind him of his duties.

Now, this would have been a good time to step back and take a look at the big picture because Guigsy can drink Liam under the table. Yet Liam is still in the bar rattling through a million and one fantastic things France needs to know about Oasis. He is still drinking seriously and still, apparently, in a great frame of mind. He is long overdue a major mood swing and I should have seen it coming.

Guigsy and I join the rest of the travelling party in the bar and polish off the last of the interviews scheduled to take place there. Our final commitment of the day is a live radio broadcast from a 'trendy' watering hole nearby – a shame, really; it had been going so well.

*   *   *

Thinking about it, what we'd been able to do in the hotel was to mould our environment to suit the band and, with hindsight, this was ever so with Oasis. Everything was always cool if Oasis or, more honestly, Liam, was given centre stage. To be fair to Liam, there is no one quite like him. He is a genuine star in a ridiculous era when weathergirls and puppet boys are similarly tagged. And, compared with his contemporaries, he shines.

* * *

At this point, Oasis are beginning to happen in France and are well-known and recognised in Paris. Certainly, the three performances I've seen them unleash here have been three of the band's best, which is to say anybody's best. Consequently, our entry to the bar for the radio broadcast is marked. Our immediate world is still sweetness and light as we are ushered politely to our table. In an effort to really bond with the surroundings, it is felt that the best champagne is the only possible choice of refreshment. The radio station is already broadcasting and, very shortly, Guigsy and Alan are back in action. The local talent is also in action, around Liam like moths to a flame, fluttering for his bacchanalian attention. Liam is never totally at ease when he is the subject of the chase, although he certainly lets a few of the better-looking girls catch him. But tonight, as on other nights, I can see that he tolerates it uneasily, rather than fully enjoys it.

Amid the buzz, Eddie Izzard arrives and sits down with one of his entourage. He is to put on his own one-man show later in the year in Paris and so has his own promotional duties, this interview included. He and I start talking, agreeing to swap guest-list favours on future occasions. Eddie is great company, both funny and self-effacing. He wears lipstick, PVC trousers and a fluorescent orange jacket. I notice that Liam finds it fairly underwhelming sitting opposite somebody sending out such an ambiguous sexual ID. This is again a long way from Burnage, Manchester. I make sure that everybody is surrounded by drinks as Liam takes his turn at the microphone. After a while, Eddie moves over to join the radio host and Liam. At first, the air is floating with pleasantries. But then Eddie begins to answer questions in half-decent French, completely charming the DJ. The spotlight is turned away from Liam and the singer's face in the shadows now reads somewhere between sullen and murder.

The first clue that all is not well in Radioland is a chair shooting backwards into a startled table of Left Bank students. They had come because they could see Sartre in Gallagher and now they have Gallagher's disoriented chair to contemplate. Liam is standing, snarling, spewing out his feelings without benefit of thought or censor. Indeed, as far as he is concerned, the world exists purely for him, a creation of his own mind: 'This isn't right . . . it's not fuckin' right . . . we're fuckin' Oasis . . . what the fuck is 'e doin' on our show? It's our fuckin' interview . . . it's not fuckin' right . . . it's on top ...' I try to calm him as he continues to spit bullets. By now the whole bar is quiet, wholly entertained. The Oasis frontman is, once again, centre stage. I ask what the problem is, but our conversation is one-sided. Liam shouts over my shoulder to Guigsy and Alan, 'Let's get out of this shit hole . . . get some serious partying done . . . bollocks to the radio... bollocks to Izzard.' But nobody is interested in going anywhere with Liam in this mood. Because of this, Liam's anger is intensifying. I put on my diplomat's cap and try to tempt him to stay calm, to leave Alan and Guigsy and to come with me to another bar to chill out. It does the trick and Liam grabs his jacket and walks with me to the door, polluting the air with a stream of invective directed at Eddie and the radio host. Alan and Guigsy also get a final jagged onslaught: 'Guigs, you fat cunt . . . White, you cunt . . . you're both on top . . . you're not in my band . . . fuck the lot of you . . . you're not fuckin' in my band . . . you don't deserve to be in Oasis . . . you can both fuck off!' This is an alcohol-induced and ill-considered verbal assault, but it is a parting shot that hits deep. I can see the wind coming out of the Oasis rhythm section's sails as we leave.

Ten minutes later, we take a table at one of Liam's favourite drinking haunts just around the corner from Lillie la Tigresse in the sleazy Pigalle district. The obligatory bottle of champagne arrives, but neither one of us feels like drinking it. Liam is still burning inside.

* * *

Point: whether Liam Gallagher is right or wrong, lucid or babbling, he is always one hundred per cent true to himself and committed to his feelings and his emotions. He is governed by them. In Paris he was deeply hurt by what had passed, and desperately upset by what *he* saw in the other two band members as disloyalty. Like I said, right or wrong? It almost doesn't matter: integrity is Liam's credo – the integrity of immediate, knee-jerk emotional response.

* * *

Our conversation isn't easy and we disagree about as much as we agree. But the worst moments seem over and I feel we are on some sort of even keel. Mentally, I relax and manage to laugh about the way things turn out — I would not feel as sanguine by the end of the evening.

Just when I thought it was safe to go back in the water, Linda finds us and joins the table. As a representative of the record company, Linda is seen as a legitimate target for Liam and he renews the verbal baiting. I make a last attempt to ditch Linda and get Liam back to the hotel without further confrontation. We would have made it if the driver hadn't insisted on waiting until Linda finished paying the bill. Now, instead of heading for the hotel, the three of us set off in an uneasy silence back to the scene of the crime. As any detective will tell you, this is a bad idea. I now give up all hope of a happy end to the evening.

As soon as the wheels of the stretch-Mercedes limousine begin to turn, Linda is again subjected to Liam's tongue-lashing. Now she's carrying the can for putting Eddie Izzard on the show. If anyone is to blame, it's the French promotion team and so I take Linda's side and try to make Liam see reason. This is a big mistake which undoes all the trust built up over the last hour. Now Liam feels he is being outflanked and falls back on his blind, menacing anger for comfort. He is boiling in a way that I have not seen before and, at forty miles per hour, throws open the car door and attempts an emergency exit. The driver hits the brakes. Linda, despairingly, lunges to hold the singer within the relative safety of the vehicle. She is unsuccessful and, as the car skids down the boulevard, Liam Gallagher is gone. I immediately leap out of the other door and roll arse-over-tit down the street. I find my feet and, dodging traffic, run over to where Liam is now dusting himself off in the real world. I check to see if he's all right, but I'm pushed away. Liam is mad for a full-on confrontation and, as I try to prevent him from disappearing without a penny in his pocket, I am jarred by a right hook to the side of my head. I am rarely surprised by anything Liam does but, in all the time I have worked with him, I've never once considered that he would strike me. I am shocked as the second blow hits me hard in the face.

My contract of employment with Oasis has thirty seconds left to run. In twelve hours Guigsy will quit the band.

I grab Liam by the lapels. I have seen active service with the Parachute Regiment and, in the heat of Arabia and the blizzards and desolation of the Arctic Circle, have operated with SAS squadrons. I have taken a lot of bullshit in the name of Queen and Country. There is only so much I can take.

Through my bitterness I know I cannot really punish the star. I pick him off his feet anyway and crash him into a nearby bus shelter. We are face-to-face but, as I look into Liam's eyes, I see only fear and confusion. I release my grip and watch as he straightens the lines of his sharp jacket and looks up at the sky. It is a gesture both powerful and pathetic. And then the parting shot that has been waiting in the wings all night: 'That's it, you're sacked . . . that's the fuckin' end for you!'

Linda has watched the entire exchange in tears and is pleading with both of us to get back in the car to pick up where we left off. Liam's shirt and jacket have been ripped in the scuffle. He stands, pale chest bared. As the street lights refract brokenly from his Elvis belt buckle, he shoots me one last look of pure hatred – animal in its intensity – before his inevitable return to the record-company security bubble. As the taillights vanish from sight, it begins to rain. I lean back against the outside of the shelter . . . totally . . . completely . . . empty.

CHAPTER 2

THE MAHARAJAH
OF RANGIPOOR

*Assuredly a man's heart is not so in his own hand,
that he can do himself all the mischief he is contented to do.*
CONJECTURA CABBALISTICA, HENRY MORE, 1653

IT WAS WEEK TWO of Parachute Regiment training. The first week had been a blur of new concepts, uniforms, information and disinformation, throughout which the training staff were polite, helpful and concerned. The screws would be tightened, they said, just a little, in week two.

A wiry little platoon sergeant, Mac French, is in the process of reviewing and inspecting my particular seven-foot-square of barracks room. He is smiling. 'We discussed the correct way to fold these shirts, Robertson, did we not?'

'Yes, Sarge,' I shout.

'Sarge? Sarge? Who the fuck are you calling Sarge? There are only two sarges in the British Army, you little knob: massarge and sausarge. I am clearly neither, unless you are on drugs. Are you on drugs, Robertson?'

'No, Sergeant.'

'Are you sure?'

'Yes, Sergeant.'

'Don't you ever call me Sarge again!'

'No, Sergeant.' I feel lucky.

'Robertson, are you a runner?'

'Yes, Sergeant.'

Sergeant French screams at Corporal Tam Noble, who stands in the doorway. 'Corporal, open the window!' Corporal Noble obeys. Sergeant French picks up my entire army belongings and barks in my face.

'Catch this, you useless cunt.'

He throws them through the open window down to the November mud three floors below. 'Can you fly, Robertson?' I feel his breath crawl up my nose.

'No, Sergeant.'

French picks up my pillows and blankets and throws them out. The mattress follows.

'Get out of my sight, Robertson.'

'Yes, Sergeant.' I walk from the room.

'Run, Robertson!'

'Yes, Sergeant.'

I run. Down the stairs, out into the mud, where my immediate world is laid, dirty and wet, beneath the grinning face of Platoon Sergeant Mac French. The screws had been tightened – just a little.

* * *

In 1972 I was twelve. The world at large, naturally, ignored this, but it was a big year for me. I bought my first record with my own money: 'Solid Gold, Easy Action' by T Rex. My father died that year.

I lived with and for rock 'n' roll pretty much every minute of every day. There were no Walkmans then, so I walked around with a Sanyo portable cassette player, listening to my favourite artists: Roxy Music; Bowie; Mott the Hoople; The Sensational Alex Harvey Band; T Rex, and the Rolling Stones. It was the Stones who reached me. This was a dangerous band, not because the press told you so. It was there in the music – twisting burned soul with a scarred heart. As soon as the Beatles shut up shop, Lennon seduced by the Oriental Pied Piper, the Rolling Stones uncoiled from behind their shadow like a king cobra. Led Zeppelin sold more records, and Lennon and McCartney had always been, arguably, better songwriters but, make no mistake, between 1969 and 1974, no finer rock 'n' roll band walked the planet than the Stones. I loved them.

Somehow, and I'm not nearly smart enough to know how, between the ages of twelve and twenty-one, I changed from a cool wee kid into a hairy-arsed, pig-biting paratrooper. Boarding school might have had something to do with it. Who knows? Perhaps one day I'll take myself to one of those Californian Jungian dream analysts – nah, why bother? It would be too little and way too late.

When I was twenty-one, I successfully completed the Parachute Regiment training and selection process. I thought I was the dog's bollocks. I was deemed by the powers-that-be fit and able to serve and protect the British Empire, or what was left of it. Keeping peace in Northern Ireland was my first tour of duty. At twenty-one, most young men are dickheads. I was no exception.

The reality of life in what is known as 'Special Forces' is hard to convey to anyone who has not lived it. It was definitely something else, some of it very, very cool. Leaping, armed to the teeth, from an aeroplane in the middle of the night into the sea was always fun. Arctic, desert and jungle survival, together with patrolling techniques learned with 22 SAS; well, looking back, all of that wasn't exactly fun. However, some fine moments came from these inhospitable landscapes. A great camaraderie establishes itself among men who share hardship. Most of our time was spent working but, when an opportunity presented itself to unwind, we did: whether it was chilling in the back of an open-topped four-ton lorry, accompanied by an ice-cold case of Tiger beer under clear Arabian night skies; or, perhaps, our own patented version of Rome's gladiatorial battles. We shared the desert with camel spiders and scorpions and, although we kidded ourselves that we were the lords of the wilderness, these were nasty, godless creatures.

On one occasion, one of my fellow troopers woke at dawn to find the fleshy part of his ear – apparently the tasty bit – missing! The *modus operandi* of the camel spider is to anaesthetise its victim before dining. In consequence, the first time you are aware that something has eaten part of you is when you look in the mirror. These spiders are as large as dinner plates, faster across the sands than a bag full of fast things and they scared the shit out of all of us. Scorpions, on the other hand, were simple to understand. They are ugly bastards, they sting you, it fucking hurts – a lot, for twenty-four hours. Despite this, we would go to great lengths to capture as many of both of these sons of bitches as we could. Having successfully entrapped them, we would then place them in pitched battle, one against the other, with a lot of hard-earned cash riding on the result. As a general rule of thumb, the scorpion would win but, on those occasions when we had a particularly large and unpleasant camel spider, it was something to see the manner in which its jaws could crush and sever the scorpion's armour plate. Not many of us slept easily after witnessing such battles.

The effect of this austere lifestyle was a kind of quickening, a test of the apprentice, where the physical and mental rigour of it all forced the man to ask questions about himself. These questions were soon to prepare me for a far more spiritual journey, to make me receptive to the subtle influence of an extraordinary friend.

While in the Parachute Regiment, I became great friends with a fellow trooper called Vivian Cook. Vivian's bearing was quiet, gentle and contemplative, but this was not a reflection of his possessing what some would consider a *girlie* name. His good nature came from that rare strength, security and knowledge found in a person who is unafraid, who is at peace with who he is, who has no need to prove anything to an ignorant world. Also, Vivian had, at one point, been a European full-contact kung-fu champion. Needless to say, his paratrooper peers were more than cautious in handling his name. Viv and

I used to spar together in the gym, 'spar' in this instance being a euphemism for his kicking the shit out of me. I just wanted to refine my already considerable killing expertise, but he saw with the eyes of a true warrior. He understood the power of avoiding conflict, even in a win situation. His aim was to guide me towards a more sanctified practice. I won't elaborate further but, if you've seen the 1970s TV series *Kung Fu,* you'll appreciate that it wasn't easy for me to hear the grasshopper at my feet in such a loud and crazy world. Without wishing to get too 'hippy' about it all, Viv's quiet guidance ensured that, during my private question-and-answer sessions later in military life, my answers took me down an increasingly civilian and, indeed, civil path.

Viv left the service of Her Majesty before I did and went to join his twin brother, Simon, as a personal security guard to Duran Duran. I, too, had by now made up my mind to return the Queen's shilling and was whiling away my last few weeks as one of Britain's soldier elite.

On a final note about our, or any other nation's, finest trained assassins, the word elite must be taken as a relative term. For example, a paratrooper is one of the best of all servicemen but, if you check out all servicemen's credentials, you'll be hard pressed to find a Nobel Prize winner among them. We could, however, from time to time, be relied upon to adjust the truth. When preparing for the passing-out parade on conclusion of Para selection, we were rehearsed in the banal questions the inspecting brigadier would inevitably ask.

*   *   *

Company Sergeant Major Lucy, playing the part of Brigadier, stops and asks me about my previous career path before my aspirations took me to the dizzy heights I had now achieved.

'I was a lifeguard, Sir,' I reply, truthfully.

'No, you were not, you lying little scumbucket!' His face turns red as he screams, 'When asked this question, you will reply, "Sir, I was a nuclear physicist," or, "Sir, I was a brain surgeon," or, "Sir, I was the Maharajah of Rangipoor, but I wanted to do something worthwhile with my life." ' He looks me up and down. 'Do you understand?'

'Yes, Sir, perfectly.' Such was regimental wit.

*   *   *

Time passed, as it will. Viv and his brother Simon turned up on the doorstep, so to speak, on my last day of service. Life outside the elite didn't look bad: they sat in a brand new steel-grey Jaguar motor car, waiting to drive me to Paris for an interview with Duran Duran.

At this point, June 1985, Duran Duran were a major act, the biggest band since, well, the last biggest band. The interview consisted of hanging out with them in Paris while keyboardist Nick Rhodes enjoyed his twenty-fifth birthday celebrations. In truth, Duran Duran was now more a memory, rather than a tightly contained unit, which had given birth to the aspirations of its various members in the shape of The Power Station and

Arcadia. Arcadia consisted of singer Simon Le Bon, Nick Rhodes and drummer Roger Taylor and they had already been in Paris for six months recording the album that would become *So Red the Rose*.

Simon and Viv had been provided with a stunning apartment in one of the more elegant parts of the city. Two days previously, I had handed back everything the British Army had ever loaned me, which was two uniforms, smart but casual, guaranteed not to stand out in a crowd. And now here I was, relaxing in deep magnolia-hide upholstery as I received my new job description from Simon.

* * *

'Stick close to the band member I nominate,' Simon says, 'but not too close. Be chilled, the guys don't appreciate heavy security.' Viv opens the well-stocked drinks cabinet and offers me a drink as Simon continues. 'When you're with them, by all means have a couple of drinks, but don't rip the arse out of it.'

'J D and Coke,' I say to Viv. I'm feeling good as he takes a bottle from the shelf.

'You'll be taxiing some of the guests from restaurant to club to club; I'd better give you a float.' Simon takes a wallet from his inside jacket pocket, pulls out a large wad of bank notes and hands it to me as if it were a business card. 'Twenty thousand francs should be enough.'

I am impressed. 'That's the equivalent of £2,500! Do you think I'll need all this?'

'This is Paris. Wives are in town. Some wives have expensive tastes. Anyway, most of the guests are leeches.'

Viv smiles as he tosses a couple of ice cubes into the Jack and Coke and hands the drink to me.

* * *

The party started in Davées, one of Nick's favourite restaurants, owned and run by a Vietnamese guy: he would constantly dab champagne behind his ears and ask Simon, Viv or myself to lick it off. Somehow, we were able to resist. As the guests began to arrive, it quickly became apparent that this would be unlike any birthday party I had ever thrown or, for that matter, attended. Le Bon, Rhodes and Roger Taylor were there with their wives, including the ridiculously attractive model Yasmin Le Bon. Mick Jagger and Ronnie Wood were in attendance, Ronnie with his wife, Jo. Mick came alone – although that was to change later. Sting came with his second wife, Trudie Styler, and – surprise, surprise – a good showing of Parisian *café society*: the so-called 'beautiful' people. Certainly nobody appeared to have been invited from the Left Bank: dog-eared paperbacks stuffed into the pockets of long overcoats were absent.

I think it would be fair to say that, as interviews go, it was not only a failure, but a complete disaster. In the first instance, my wardrobe had not, while in the Army, expanded to accommodate the rather eccentric fashion dictates of New Romanticism – my wardrobe had rarely stayed in my room long enough with Mac French around to accommodate anything. In a room full of peacocks, I stood out like a bulldog's bollocks. And then there was the far from small matter that I was completely and utterly in awe. Mick Jagger and Ronnie Wood! Mick Jagger! There was little likelihood that I would remain 'chilled' as Simon had suggested I should be. At one particular club, where I was meant to be casually checking for Nick Rhodes, who was with Jagger, I became a starstruck statue, rooted to the floor, transfixed as if all were a hallucination.

I topped off an already inauspicious evening while driving in convoy with Simon. He had with him Nick Rhodes and Roger and Giovanna Taylor. I had Jo Wood and Julie Anne Rhodes with me. We came to a stop at a roundabout, my vehicle just behind Simon's. Rather hilariously, I thought, I tried to shunt his vehicle gently into the oncoming traffic. Had it, in fact, been gentle, maybe it would have been passed off as just one more cock-up by Viv's clueless mate. Unfortunately, my foot slipped on the clutch and we hurtled into the back of Simon's Jag. The VIP passengers' frightened heads turned and stared back at me. All I could do was laugh nervously which, undoubtedly, gave the impression of some congenital manic disorder. No one else laughed. Later, Simon explained that I had just failed the world's most relaxed selection process.

Jagger had a better night than I did. At some point along the evening's trail of entertainment, the more serious party animals brought a shambolic close to the revels in Nick Rhodes' apartment. All lightweights had given up the ghost, leaving for wherever was home for the night. Jagger, one of the first guests to arrive, was still looking sharp. As soon as we entered Nick's latest purchase, an enormous serviced apartment opposite the Plaza Athenée Hotel in the most *frou-frou* fragment of a *chi-chi* city (Nick's neighbour was Marlene Dietrich — enough said), a grown-up version of the old schoolyard favourite, kiss-chase, was drawn to resolution. Two blonder-than-blonde Scandinavian party accessories had sought to attract Mick's attention and, throughout the night, he was doing just enough to keep them in line. Now he circled in earnest, shark-like, charm turned up to eleven.

The circles drew tighter as smiles grew brighter. This sly dog won't bark, just bite. The flaxen-haired nymphettes were loving it. They had OD'd on celebrity and champagne. The aloof and distancing messages they had sent out on arrival – in sheer silk that ran tightly around taut, tanned teenage skin – had evaporated, as alcohol combined with occasion. The young goddesses had inhaled long and hard the atmosphere around the assembled stars: if it were helium, they would have made Pinky and Perky sound deep. Mick undressed the problem of choice simply – he chose both. As the three of them slipped into the white marble bathroom, it was noticeable that, although the girls giggled, for Jagger, the smiling had stopped.

They clearly had a great deal to discuss in there; it was many minutes before the trio re-emerged. My money's on Mick as a skilful and practised storyteller. His young companions were red-faced and laughing. Dresses were a little awry; strands of hair had been released from artful bondage. Jagger, on the other hand, remained unmoved. The smile, though, was back. And wider than ever.

Although, on this occasion, I travelled home to join the unemployed, by exaggerating my involvement with the Duran clan, I miraculously managed to secure more work within the music industry. Simon and Viv once again helped and set me up with Spandau Ballet. Then followed Sigue Sigue Sputnik, the Sisters of Mercy, ex-Thin Lizzy's Gary Moore and Public Image Limited. Suddenly, I realised I knew what I was doing, what was expected of me, and I became comfortable with it. I was given the chance to work as a tour manager, looking after the Quireboys, Emerson Lake and Palmer and BBM (Jack Bruce and Ginger Baker of Cream fame, and Gary Moore). And along the way, I had the great privilege to be a part of both Nelson Mandela tributes at Wembley Stadium.

I ran into Mick Jagger and Ronnie Wood again, only this time on a more professional basis as both they and Charlie Watts were part of a blues festival that I played a part in co-ordinating. The starstruck awe had now gone but, when Jagger lurched into 'Going Down' by Freddie King, something connected between heaven and earth and danced up my spine and it was easy to see where the voodoo came from, a legacy passed down through generations from blues singer and guitarist Robert Johnson. Mick's performance of some of the classics that gave him the need to sing was mesmerising.

Over a period of time, I got to work with blues legends like Buddy Guy, Pops Staples, Jimmy Rogers, Otis Rush and Albert Collins and found myself sharing dinner tables with the likes of George Harrison, a real live Beatle.

The Parachute Regiment's motto is *utrinque paratus*, meaning 'ready for anything'. In the topsy-turvy world of rock 'n' roll, I thought I was. But around the corner lay Oasis – will I never learn?

CHAPTER 3

HAIL, HAIL, ROCK 'N' ROLL

And what rough beast, its hour come round at last,
Slouches towards Bethlehem to be born?
'THE SECOND COMING', W. B. YEATS

HOW GOOD ARE OASIS?

Ever ridden on a rollercoaster? Think about the point when, having reached for the heavens, the carriage turns back towards where *you* live – for one glorious fraction of a fraction of a second, weightlessness kicks in...

They're that good.

I saw them live for the first time in New York City in July 1994 in a dank ordinary club called Wetlands on the lower-west side of Manhattan. The music industry's much-trumpeted New Music Seminar was in full swing and, as part of a programme of live shows, creative workshops, discussion groups and guest speakers, there was this Oasis gig at the club. They weren't even headlining: an inadequate and forgettable band called Moist wasted that opportunity. First on the bill were X-CNN (this was my professional reason for being in town). Oasis were sandwiched between them.

The buzz about Oasis had already begun in the UK. In America it was a whole different ball game; the only people really aware of the band's existence were industry insiders. Despite this, the ripple from across the Atlantic was strong enough to generate a wave of anticipation for what was to come. I was as keen as anybody else to see the new future of British rock 'n' roll, this being the tag they had already picked up from the UK music press. I'd heard their first two chart singles, 'Supersonic' and 'Shakermaker', many times on radio and knew that they were far more than an echo of the earlier baggy scene, as some pundits were hinting.

I was staying at the Paramount, the same hotel as this self-assured posse from Manchester. The interior of the hotel was the work of Philippe Starck, the highly regarded designer/artist whose furniture wouldn't look out of place in an S&M den. The Paramount Hotel is a Mecca of supercool, an aesthetic triumph of style over substance. Try shaving in one of the washbasins, or sitting on one of the toilets – Rodin's Thinker could forget stroking his chin, as he'd have needed both hands to steady his arse. The Paramount also came with Armani-clad designer staff: striking good looks, but all sharing one brain.

The day before the Wetlands show, I had seen a familiar face across the hotel's sparse curving lobby. It was Marcus Russell. Marcus and I had met for the first time four years earlier when he was managing The The; Simon Cook, as their road manager, had introduced me. Marcus was now the manager of Oasis.

Simon had prepared the ground between Marcus and myself when the three of us rounded off a totally scandalous drinking session at Simon's apartment in Muswell Hill, north London. Out came the Rebel Yell and we talked, lied, stumbled and mumbled way into the night, playing whatever CD fell from the rack, discovering a mutual appreciation for Steve Earle and, not surprisingly, the Stones. En route from that night to our meeting as accidental tourists in a spartan lobby, we had seen each other perhaps three, maybe four, times. But it would be fair to say that we were already friends.

Marcus Russell is a good guy by any standard you care to set. Not that any Hollywood producer would be crazy enough to cast him but, in the language of an early Western, he'd be the guy in the white hat. As much as the Paramount is a triumph for style over everything, Marcus Russell is the opposite, as unremarkable in appearance as he is cool-headed and able when and where it counts. More importantly, he actually cares about what he does, about the artist . . . about the music.

As we crossed the lobby to exchange surprised greetings, I finally found a function for Starck's hotel: alienation makes the heart grow fonder. It felt good to see him. Although we both had commitments, we arranged to get together for a couple of drinks after the show.

* * *

The Wetlands is not much to look at. It's in a shitty part of town that looks like it was always a shitty part of town which is never going to grow up amounting to much. On a viciously hot and humid New York City afternoon, having hailed the only yellow cab around without the benefit of refrigeration, I'm sweating like a bastard. Unfortunately, the radio does work and Sting is telling me what it's like to be an Englishman in New York. I am having a serious sense-of-humour failure and, despite the surrounding decay, am so pleased to arrive. Inside, I taste the air-conditioned dry shadows of the culture that gave birth to cool, dark pool halls and cold beer. God bless America . . . God bless Air Con.

It is the time of day that, in a certain world, is reserved for the soundcheck. Each band in the evening's line up is given an opportunity to test the venue's acoustics and, in theory, to iron out any foreseeable problems in the balance between band-sound and building. Things are going well if the singer can be heard and the bass and snare drums don't sound like a pillow and a tin of biscuits. Only the headline act get all the time they need and the rest make do and hope that their sound engineer can pull it together at showtime — in truth, most can't. Today is no exception, each band trying to jam sixty minutes into the half an hour, the twenty minutes, or even the ten minutes that they are begrudgingly given.

Having arrived punctually, I am with X-CNN in the dressing room staring at the desperately unfunny graffiti, a legacy of other nights and other bands. We can't soundcheck until Oasis have soundchecked, and Oasis have not arrived. When they finally do, true to their reputation, no hint of apology is offered. This doesn't seem unduly rude, and certainly there is no malice; it is evidence merely of their 'divine right' to do what they want when they want.

WHAT'S THE STORY?

This is when I hear Liam's scathing, elastic vocal in the flesh for the first time. I see his mouth open, the sinews at the front of his neck tightening as his hands clench white-knuckled behind his back. This is a sound from the street, of not having but wanting . . . a martial challenge. With none of the sweetness of Noel's rich, melodic guitar to temper and balance its violence, it is a brutal thing, and it is breathtaking. Liam's voice has been described by many as 'Lennon-meets-Lydon' but defies such a lazy comparison. Liam Gallagher sounds like Liam Gallagher. It's almost unbelievable to think that it took him the best part of twenty years to realise that the voice is there.

Liam Gallagher. Born 21st September 1972. VIRGO. There are Virgos out there who are so terrified of taking risks that they would rather be boiled in Clorox than touch anything sticky. They go to work, come home, go to work, come home, living out their entire non-existence doing the ant thing. Don't let that happen to you! With Uranus now moving into your 6th house, you must try to worry less about getting a gold watch and a pension plan, and just go ahead and leap fearlessly into new work. Healthwise, why not try something new there also, instead of pretending you already know it all? (Planetarium by Michael Lutin in *Vanity Fair*, May 1994.)

Maybe that's why it will not wait to be heard now. As I watch him rant into the mic, I bet he couldn't keep it in if he wanted to. Coming out of Detroit city in 1968, the MC5, the world's first punk band, were kicking out the jams; Oasis just want to kick out your teeth. I know right then and there that I want to be in their gang.

* * *

If you weren't at the gig at the Wetlands — unlucky. I was, and Oasis were all the things a great band should be: arrogant and dismissive of all, save the job at hand. They nailed my skull to the back of the venue and performed brutal surgery with a set that lasted no longer than it takes to travel from Manchester's scarred inner suburbs to the brighter lights of the city centre on a Saturday night. That night in Manhattan they shone like you and I probably never will. All who lined the sweating walls of the club realised that the night was special – cynics and fans alike. The Devil was in the house and, you know what? He really does have all the best tunes.

There was, however, one moment that signalled the inimical essence of Liam. To reach the stage, the band had to walk a dark artery from the dressing room, a passage that allowed for one--way traffic only. They were forced to pass Marcus, who was waiting to wish them well, and all smiled in appreciation of this small gesture — all that is except Liam who, in a sudden movement with nothing of the playground in it, pushed the manager to one side.

Later, Marcus and I had that drink and a few more besides, along with Bonehead from Oasis, in a quiet corner of the Paramount's hip bar, the Whisky. I knew I wanted to work with this band, although, as far as my career was concerned, it would be a retrograde step as the only opening was likely to be within the security operation. But I wanted the job out of instinct, not for my CV. In fact, I wanted the job so much I became repetitive in my insistence of suitability. If you don't ask, you don't get. I flew home the next morning with a hangover that would have killed most people.

Two weeks later, my girlfriend brought me the news that I knew would give me my chance. At an Oasis gig in Newcastle, for no reason other than jealous ignorance, a no-neck, no-brain, no-hope rent-a-thug had leaped onstage and punched Noel in the eye, shattering his perma-place sunglasses and, with that blow, shattering any illusions anyone might have had that because they were on stage they were safe. On paper, the deal is simple: band plays, punter pays. No one in the band expects to have to spend quality time with individual members of the audience in mid-performance! When this demarcation is blurred, it is unnerving for the performer and time to enforce the difference between musician and wannabe.

So I got the call I was hoping for: another 'lazy rock 'n' roll interview', only this time I knew my act was together.

CHAPTER 4

STOLEN
AND STORED

He's your street guru? Well, I'll take my kippers and go.
MY LANDLADY, BARBARA MEEKING, 14 JANUARY 1996

MY FIRST OFFICIAL MEETING WITH OASIS is at the Astoria Theatre in August 1994, in distinct contrast to sipping bourbon while receiving a Duran Duran brief amid the alleged glamour of Paris. The Astoria was just off London's crass retail centre of consumer mediocrity, Oxford Street, near the junction with Tottenham Court Road, where disposable hopes slip into the gutter along with the interminable flysheets handed out by the student-hungry English-language centres. It's a grubby, monochrome sort of day, a shroud of dampness draped over everything. Marcus had arranged to meet me outside the theatre. As it happens, we arrive together. Noel and Liam are with him, the three having just strolled up Charing Cross Road, unmolested: a prospect that will become unthinkable in the months ahead.

This was the moment for a first real take on Noel and Liam. It is peculiar to young men in hip bands that, unprompted, they will never remember your having first met them: they are far more concerned with making, rather than receiving, impressions. The one exception to this, actually proving the rule, is when they meet someone more famous than they are. The super super-duper star, in turn, will not remember first meeting them. File this law and apply it always in your dealings with icons and apprentice icons – it will soften the blow their blank gaze bestows. It's nothing personal; it's a DNA thing. So, as is the law, Noel and Liam made their impressions on me. In that first sixty seconds, they were warm, open and seemed genuinely pleased to meet me and, for what it's worth, they looked fantastic. At this point in their career, there were not vast sums of money available to squander on appearances. Despite this, they were both double sharp: boot-cut Levis over Adidas trainers; a plain navy crewneck for Noel; a sloppy chilled-out Adidas tracksuit for Liam. Both wore what were, even then, trademark shades, their hair in borrowed Beatle-esque fringes flopping down to meet these dark windows. I have to admit, I'm a sucker for bands that look like bands. They had clearly adopted the Inspiral Carpets' 'Cool as Fuck!' legend as essential doctrine.

* * *

We four now move away from the cheap lingerie shops into the more inviting darkness of the theatre. It is a labyrinthine place, but I am able to navigate through its maw having done a number of shows there with other bands. We arrive at the Astoria's heart to witness the crew lazily setting up for the soundcheck.

The other three band members are there already: bass player Paul McGuigan, known to all as Guigsy; rhythm guitarist Paul Arthurs, aka Bonehead; and the band's original drummer, Tony McCarroll, a man loved by one and all. They are skilfully demonstrating their ability with a football, a talent as natural to them as the licking of its own testicles is to the family dog. The volleys of abuse that pass as greetings in the Oasis camp are exchanged. From this, I gather that no one can be sure who or where their fathers are.

Paul Arthurs. Born 23 June 1965. CANCER. With Uranus at your solar 8th-house cusp, what you can't do is second-guess the wild card in the deck – life itself.

Paul McGuigan. Born 9 May 1971. TAURUS. Whether you're a posh tourist cruising on a windy sea, a computer hacker crashing somebody else's Windows in a windowless office, or a soldier trying to stay cool when your CO blows up right in front of you, spontaneity must become your guiding principle now.

Alan White. Born 26 May 1972. GEMINI. Anybody who dares to limit your thinking from now on is in big trouble. (Planetarium by Michael Lutin in *Vanity Fair*, May 1994.)

The band is now together, and together they are a gang. Guigsy, Bonehead and Tony are as artlessly and effortlessly clad as their ringleaders in casual combinations of Burberry and Marks & Spencer that were never intended as the last word in street style. In some faceless corporate den just around the corner, a gaggle of marketing professionals will surely wade into celebratory champagne, unable to believe their good fortune.

*　*　*

Marcus chose a moment to take me to one side and discuss what was required that day. The safety of the performing artist is generally ensured by severely restricted access, so that anyone who is not directly concerned with putting on the show should have no chance of penetrating the artist's safety screen. Inevitably, there will always be a more persistent element to any crowd. Once in Detroit, when touring with the Sisters of Mercy, I was offered $1,000 in cash for my 'Access All Areas' tour pass. Fortunately, I am as honest as the day is long and passed on the offer – that's my story, your honour, and I'm sticking to it. Away from the structured environs of performance, the artist is cushioned by the presence of security personnel. He or she relies on their minder's ability to discern whether or not an exchange with the real world is welcome. At the point where a correct assessment is made, and the artist needs to be extricated from an over-zealous fan who just knows that the last album was all about them and their life, this exercise must be conducted with maximum diplomacy.

Nobody welcomes brutal security and the worst offenders

are often the thugs many promoters or venues supply as 'house security'. Almost exclusively, those lucky enough to be employed directly by an artist have, over a period of time, displayed wit enough to conduct themselves with grace under fire. I did, of course, say almost exclusively. I recall one Swedish slab of testosterone who was working for the late guitar virtuoso Gary Moore. During a European tour, this Viking throwback decided to do a little freelance pillaging. Crashing into the area of the gig reserved for the disabled, he ripped a camera from a young girl in a wheelchair and tore the film from it. Amazingly, he was delighted by his own vigilance. The next thing he had in his hand was his P45, and rightly so.

I forget whose idea it was, but lunch and a cup of tea was suggested. This took everybody to catering. Somehow, Cat and Mouse – purveyors of fine chip butties by appointment to Oasis – had transformed a very ordinary room into a truckers' cafe with a riot of gingham and more than a touch of sauce (HP, of course). I was the new kid in town and contented myself with sitting quietly and watching.

A lot has been made of the constant enmity that seems to characterise Noel and Liam's relationship. Sure enough, within an hour of having formally made their acquaintance, the Gallagher brothers squared up to each other. The discussion they were having over fried chicken and chips became an argument, escalated into a row and chewed and ground its way towards a screaming match. I can't remember what it was about: I think a return to an earlier Gallagher versus Gallagher debate regarding the validity of Lennon, alive in 1995. One thing was for sure, volume was the only currency with any value. Liam shouts because these issues are desperately important to him; Noel shouts because Liam is shouting. The response of the immediate camp is to shake their heads, laugh and order refills of strong, sweet tea. The performance ended as Liam swept from the room, reminding me of the Tasmanian Devil cartoon character, only better dressed. Somehow the standard soundcheck still had to go down, together with a trip to the MTV studios, before they returned to play the sold-out gig to 2,000 ticket holders.

* * *

As the band minus Liam take the stage to begin the check, I tuck myself into a dark corner. The guys are flying through 'Supersonic'. Engineer Mark Coyle, doing his best to bring order to a cacophony of sound, has his finger firmly on the button marked loud. Liam is needed to complete the mix. He emerges from the gloom and now stands in front of the stage, listening in judgement, waiting to add his essential violence.

'Liam.' It is an invitation from Coyle to the dance, and he doesn't need asking twice.

Powering forward, he leaps from ground level clean to the stage four feet above and, with a malevolent glance at Noel (ignored), he now squares up to the mic. Silence from the band. Just Liam, Liam alone. The first line of the song 'Shakermaker' scythes through the room. A few more lines on his own and then the group crashes in with him. Another couple of bars and Liam pulls away from the mic, mouthing something undetectable to

Noel who, in response, steps out of his own groove to take up the challenge. Without them the music is lost and gropes its way blindly to a stuttering halt. It's fight night and the brothers top the bill . . . again. Offstage, all that can be heard is confused. And Liam is gone, leaving angry, empty space.

*   *   *

I knew I didn't have any part to play in the band dynamic this early on, so I decided to meet the permanent crew. Mark Coyle first, front-of-house soundman, a lean, rangy individual, eternally squinting at the world. Trying to martial his ever-diminishing eyesight to detect movement and colour clearly more than four feet away, he resolutely refused to wear spectacles. Phil Smith, backline technician and black-belt-third-dan in the ancient art of sleeping, moves like there isn't a bone in his body that is actually connected, and is never far away from a spliff. And, finally, Jason Rhodes, temporary production manager and Noel's guitar tech, a hard-faced ex-rugby league player whose capacity for substance abuse became a source of wide-eyed wonder. My first impression of the crew? Not one of them that day filled me with confidence but, as I was to learn as we journeyed around the world, each, in his way, was as solid as rock.

*   *   *

The stand-offs between Noel and Liam are marked by the speed at which they are later reconciled with each other. As the two of them, along with Bonehead and myself, slip out of the stage door at the rear of the venue, it's all smiles. Outside in the narrow street that connects the Astoria with Soho, two down-at-heel Ford Granadas, ashtrays on wheels, are waiting to ferry us to MTV. Along for the ride is the Coyle and Paul Slattery. All bands attract satellites, a nucleus of individuals orbiting celebrity, attracted only by the cosy glow of refracting spotlight. Slattery spins with the best of them, a freelance photographer whose credentials are provided by his earlier visual documentation of British heroes The Smiths.

Our car pulls away with myself in the front. Slattery has wormed his way between Noel and Liam in the back, even though there is space aplenty in the car behind. Before we nose out into the Charing Cross Road, the sales pitch has begun, as always, with praise.

'You guys are for real,' wheedles the photographer. 'I could tell that right from the beginning, like The Smiths, the first time I saw you, I knew.' As we jerk our way to Camden Town in the weight of London's late-afternoon traffic, he reaches his point. 'I should definitely travel to Japan with you. You're at a stage where documentary evidence of what's happening is essential – it's a record for your benefit, not mine.'

Noel stares out through the side window, grunting in non-committal response. Liam is a more malleable target for such entreaties.

'Fucking right, Slats, you're on it. Noel, we've got to tell Marcus . . . Slats is coming.'

Watching this exchange through the compacted field of vision that a cracked rearview mirror affords, I see Noel's eyes roll. We pull up outside MTV. Super.

We're inside, a gang again, Bonehead and the Coyle joining Noel and Liam, Slattery two steps behind. We pass the paunchy security and sign in. This visit is still a new and novel experience for Oasis. Later, attitudes to promotional activity will change. Right now, they're mad for it.

Turn right on entering . . . move through the open-plan reception . . . cosy up in the guest suite. The response en route indicates that a good number of the station's employees don't recognise their guests. Noel turns to me as the afternoon schedule is being explained. 'Robbo, we did *Top of the Pops* yesterday and it's on tonight . . . the same time as we're meant to be filming this MTV thing . . . can somebody make sure I get a recording?' Noel gives the impression that he is talking to his fingertips, only making eye contact when his sentence is finished.

Liam and Bonehead overhear: 'Fucking hell, yeah!' A chorus of excited support for Noel's proposal. The freshness of these days is clear to see and infectious to be around. I rattle a few cages to ensure the necessary equipment will be in place. I'm now as vibed up as they are about watching this early appearance on the show that has always been emerging talent's own benchmark of success.

Noel looks around, surveying the contemporary media centre that is to become his band's kingdom in the eighteen months to come. But today he is looking backwards. He points to an unsightly blemish on a nearby wall: 'There used to be a very expensive sculpture there.' There had been until the band Primal Scream and its wake washed through some months earlier. Noel had been part of that entourage: twenty or so young guns riding in on wings of speed, coke and smack, each to his own, bringing with them a little mayhem as souvenirs of the visit. Now Noel is here on his own terms, with his own burgeoning band of misfits, intent on tasting the sweetness of the moment.

The guest suite, hospitality lounge, what you will, is as charmless and unimaginative as these places often are. Like the part of the British Airways lounge where they give you free biscuits for flying business class, a teaser of the opulence in the first-class sanctuary behind the protective moat of smoked glass, beyond which silver buckets nurse the good stuff.

Still, there is enough soft black leather to swallow all of us. It's Miller Time and our MTV gopher scurries to fill a detailed list – too much to drink, please!

'Anybody got a mobile phone?' Noel wants to know. A phone surfaces. 'Pass it here.' He dials a familiar number and soon his words ricochet off the ionosphere. Ever wondered where the echoes of the words of all the conversations on these portable people links go?

* * *

STRANGE DIALOGUE IN SPACE

ALEISTER CROWLEY:

hersnoutforthequarrysetfleshyandheavy-
andgrossbestialbrokenacrossandbelow-
ithermouththatdripsbloodfromthelipst-
hathidethefangsofthesnakedripsonven-
omousuddersmountainousflanksthat-
fretandthespiritsickensandshuddersat-
thehintofaworsethingyet.

NOEL GALLAGHER:
Erm, just a couple of grams will be fine.

Diary of a Drug Fiend was Aleister Crowley's first published novel. To the reader of 1922 it presented a shocking look at a little-known phenomenon... The book was written by Crowley after years of deep personal study and experimentation with drugs... It will also prove a useful document to doctors, lawyers, police and addicts for its unique and precise presentation of the psychology of addiction. (From the cover notes of the 1985 reprint of Aleister Crowley's *Diary of a Drug Fiend*.)

Aleister Crowley quote taken from
1922 edition of *Diary of a Drug Fiend*

Another list is drawn up. Pharmaceuticals – nothing Boots the Chemist can supply – are on their way.

A drinks trolley is wheeled in laden with Becks, gin, vodka and mixers. Gravity pulls on a mountain of ice barely contained by an imitation silver bucket. Light appears to strike diamonds in the bright highball glasses and I swear they whisper 'Fill me, drink from me, fill me again.' Have I seen too many Martini commercials? Right now, it seems silly not to listen. A blurring of fact and fantasy. What's the worst that could happen? A neurotic yuppy white rabbit consults its watch – like there's something important to do? But this is work, honestly, and Ray Cokes's harrassed producer is ready for a camera rehearsal: 'Can I have the band, please?'

Sure she can. Noel, Liam and Bonehead obligingly file into the house-of-fun that is the set of MTV's *Most Wanted*. Instruments are picked up. Noel takes a twelve-string acoustic guitar, Bonehead some kind of weird Bontempi-style organ thing and Liam, mic, mic, Liam. Pleased to meet you, hope you guessed my name. An impromptu chorus, unknown to all, is kicked into life by Noel singing, 'We were on *Top of the Pops*, we were on *Top of the Pops* . . . and we did not wear flip flops.' Liam's eyes flash in good humour, a look of understanding and warmth towards big brother. He dazzles everybody with a smile that is full of magic. These are definitely better days. Schmaltzy? I was there: that's how it was.

Ray Cokes is on holiday, so Davina McCall stands in. She's a babe and someone to flirt with. She giggles and laughs and lets us get on with it. Because she's so chilled, the boys do just that.

The camera operators aren't the only ones who need to

rehearse. The song isn't ready. It's a halfling, almost stillborn, pulled unrealised from whatever *sensei* nourish Noel. We all know now where the song will take the writer, and where the writer leaves the song.

Finished? A song is never finished . . . it's abandoned.

Even so, the wonder . . . the stripped-down acoustic tones of the new song, 'Whatever', unveil themselves to show an intuitive grasp of what a song should be, and all in the studio are taken in, conned by the trite whimsy of its hippy lyric.

This moment recalls McCartney sharing the experience of being woken early one morning as the milkman whistles. The Beatles were number one and McCartney's tune, having travelled the world, was returning home. Whatever, Noel, it's your turn now.

With the rehearsal over, we are now back in the hostility lounge. There's drinking to be done and surely more laughter to come . . . and there's a new face. In front of us is a blonde with rock chick practically tattooed across her forehead. Nice dress she nearly got into: cleavage spills across the room. But she's definitely got something . . . she's the 'it' girl . . . it's a bag of something . . . something light, something white, something to ruin your appetite . . . let's hear it for Charlie . . . welcome aboard.

The plump little plastic wrap arcs through the air towards Coyley: crap eyesight or no, he makes a catch Atherton would kill for. As an outfielder, I move to the door, push it open six inches or so to ensure that nobody will see this who doesn't need to. Coyle is working in practised fashion with admirable economy of movement. White lines are carved and groomed across the glass table – smoked glass – we're all riding first-class now.

I have observed in all parts of the *West Indies*, where I have been, that the natives delight in holding herbs, roots, or twigs in their mouths. Thus, in the territory of *Antiocha*, they use a small Herb, called Coca, and other sorts in the province of *Arma*. In those of *Quimbaya* and *Anzerma*, they cut twigs off a sort of tender middling tree, which is always green, wherewith they are incessantly rubbing their teeth. (From *The Seventeen Years' Travels of Pedro de Cieza de Leon through the Mighty Kingdom of Peru*, Pedro de Cieza de Leon, 1532–50.)

Snorters gather hungrily around the trough, snouts twitching for the feast: fine Columbian cuisine, plenty for everyone. Crisp bank notes are rolled into tight tubes, ready for a nasal vacuum cleaning. The Bank of England's representatives, Dingley Dell and All Muggleton, step to the crease. It's an away fixture with South America. Dickens watches – that's Charles Dickens, but you can call me Charlie. Sure enough, there is plenty, but not for me. Not that I never have, not that I never will . . . this is work . . . I'm being paid. There's fun to be had watching others play in the snow.

In most parts about *Cali* and *Popayan*, they hold in their mouths the aforesaid small *Coca*, with a composition they keep in little calabashes, or else a sort of earth, like lime.

Throughout all Peru, from the time they rise in the morning till they go to bed at night, they are never without this Coca in their mouths. The reason some *Indians*, to whom I put the question, gave me for doing so was that it made them insensible of hunger, and added to their strength and vigour. Something there may be in it, yet I am rather of the opinion it is only an ill habit, and fit for such people as they are. (As before, Pedro de Cieza de Leon, 1532–50.)

STOLEN AND STORED

Time is flying – in fact, just about everyone's flying – and now it's showtime. A rare synchronous moment takes place as the band breeze through 'Live Forever' for MTV coincides with the group's two-dimensional soundbyte on BBC1 – Oasis are on *Top of the Pops*! As arranged, the moment is stolen and stored on VCR. Not Andy Warhol's fifteen minutes of fame, this, no, this is just a beginning. We head back to the suite, which now looks a little more lived-in. Roll VT, Liam cringes, the others laugh. It must be said, there have been better vocal deliveries of the song.

In periphery, a white rabbit: yes, there's an important date. Dusty Granadas trail red lights back through a city changing out of its suit, back to the Astoria, back to where the band's soul is tonight, back to live.

Everyone talking, no one listening, everything louder than everything else – c'mon!

Five minutes to curtain, four minutes, three, two, one...

The roar of the crowd when the band ooze on to the stage ices skin . . . nerve endings . . . my entire system. What must it be like when you're the target? Dream on.

'Liam! Liam! Liam!' The little girls at the front cry for attention, recognition, acknowledgement of their existence. He gives it. Eyes make contact.

Tonight he's a rock 'n' roll star. And for tonight and last night, and what he is giving, and for that voice, and the music. History will afford him that status too: it is being written in stone. Tomorrow, well, that's tomorrow, eh? Let Rome in Tiber melt and the wide arch of the ranged empire fall! Here is my space; Kingdoms are clay.

Exhausted now, the band is slumped in the dull, cold dressing room. Drinks are their nurses, while punters spill out into the clammy carbon monoxide that pretends to be air. They seem happy. They got their money's worth; Oasis got their money. A party beckons at the Leisure (lizard) Lounge. On the way out, Noel shows he knows his place and mine: 'Robbo, make sure these get back to the hotel.' Black Hush Puppies are passed to me. Oddly, this request tells me that my interview is going well, as these guys don't entrust their Hush Puppies to just anybody.

We can walk to the Leisure Lounge from the Astoria, and we do. As we arrive at the door, a crush sways like a headache choreographed by David Byrne. I chop a route out for the band and we pass down the stairs to be met with the biting riff of Primal Scream's 'Rocks'. I float about the place, trying to keep an eye on my wards for the night, hung out on a line (it is late, might be better if I were).

'Great party, isn't it?' Noel's at my shoulder. It isn't really a great party and he knows it. But it's his party . . . it's jammed . . . everyone wants in. Outside, many stand cold and envious.

Meanwhile, Liam's night is being ruined by a petite, sexy, wild-eyed blonde, all curves and high heels; a feather boa tickles her tits. She and Liam are screaming at each other. This, apparently, is Cerisse, Liam's girlfriend. Her *raison d'être* has been to crawl into his head; everyone saw it but Liam; it took a brother to give him the good news. I know none of this; it's just another shouting match to me. Cerisse is finding out how difficult it is for the new *face* to focus all his attention on the one pussy. Non-pc? I just call it the way I see it.

Liam and I leave. The party will inevitably fade to the usual sad, slow end, no-hopers finding hope in dragging out an evening, sniffing for some final excitement before they open their eyes to another day older and deeper in debt. Noel, naturally, had left at just the right moment a couple of hours earlier – one who instinctively knows when something is right.

We've lost Cerisse. I speak too soon – there she goes, there she goes again, as we hit the pavement. She's back, she shouts, Liam wants none of it.

'But I've got no money.' Cerisse is now whimpering and even the feather boa looks embarrassed. 'How can I get home with no money? Bastard!'

As I said, I didn't know the history of the relationship, but it obviously had no future. Digging into my pocket, I find and pull out two ten-pound notes. I'm tempted to push them down the front of her dress, but that doesn't seem right. 'Here, money.' I press the notes into her hand. 'Now fuck off!' Cerisse seems stunned; she's certainly silent. We leave her staring at the cash, and at us, and at the cash, as Liam cackles and skips along the road. He reminds me of Brer Rabbit, off to find his laughing place. All that's needed is a giant animator's pencil-eraser to rub out the London skyline and draw him in dungarees on a dusty lane climbing up to a Southern Technicolor sunset. We're gone.

*   *   *

A hotel room in west London, 10:00 am. The phone rings. I pick it up: 'Robbo, they love you.'

'What? Who loves me?' I'm not used to such early-morning affection.

'It's Marcus. The guys think you're top.'

'Top?'

'Noel and Liam reckon you'll do. You're in.'

I sit up. Sunshine and fresh coffee. 'Great! What's next?'

'The band are off to Japan and America...'

'Brilliant!'

'But I can't afford to take you on this one.'

'Oh.' Clouds; the coffee's instant.

'However, when they get back, you're in. I'll catch up with you soon.'

I put the phone down and make my way to the bathroom. How rare, and how wonderful: a hotel bath more than big enough to stretch out in and savour the moment. It fills, clean steam rises, I'm smiling.

A little patience never hurt anybody.

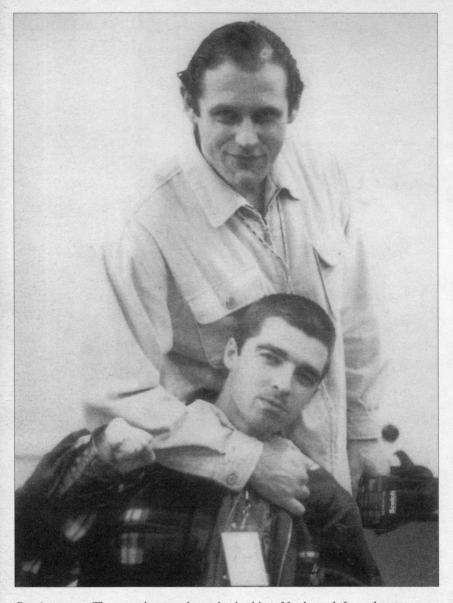

Previous page: The amazing two-legged grin thing -Noel, top left- and spars
(from top) Liam Gallagher, Alan White, Paul McGuigan and Bonehead.
Club Citta, Kawaski, 22 August 1995.   *(© Mitch Ikeda)*.

Above: Noely G and the author: backstage at Southampton, 30 November 1994.
                                              (© Paul Slattery).

Opposite: "Are you looking at my pint?" Club Citta.   *(© Mitch Ikeda.)*

Club Citta *(As before. © Mitch Ikeda).*

Above: Mark Coyle (*centre*), sound engineer and long-time friend of the band. Backstage at the rave at Eagles, Milwaukee, 25 March 1995.

Below: Preparing for the video shoot for "Whatever" – crew members Phil (*left*), Jason and Noel (*centre*).

Above: Noel busks as Guigs and Melissa, our US merchandisers observe. He received less than the price of a pint. Mesa, Arizona, 5 February 1995.

Below: Taken in the Gents at First Avenue Club, Minneapolis owned by The Artist Formerly Known As Prince, 24 March 1995.

Above: Noel obliges in photo opportunity, Mesa, Arizona- manager Marcus Russell looks on, 1st February, 1995.

Below: A million miles from nowhere, crew member Jason, Marcus and Bonehead on board the silver roadhog, Somewheresville, USA 1995.

CHAPTER 5

DIALOGUES

SCENE 1

DRAMATIS PERSONAE

MARCUS RUSSELL:	Manager of Oasis.
IAIN ROBERTSON:	Tour manager and security co-ordinator.
ABBY:	Marcus Russell's personal assistant.

THE LONDON BASED OFFICES OF IGNITION, *the management company looking after the rock group Oasis. The space is functional, perhaps a little cramped: there are more working bodies than there are desks. The phone rings constantly, cutting harshly through the hive of activity. Framed silver and gold discs, and magazine covers featuring the band, are scattered, not hung, about the floor. A clock reads 10:00 am. One desk is separate from the chaos. A bottle of aspirin sits in the middle of this desk. Next to it is a fax with URGENT stamped across the top and bottom. Also separate sits* IAIN ROBERTSON, *clearly a visitor. Suddenly, a door opens and a stocky man in his early forties,* MARCUS RUSSELL, *enters looking worried. He sees* IAIN *and forces a smile. He heads for the empty desk, sits and prises open the top of the aspirin bottle.*

ABBY: Can I get you a coffee?

MARCUS: No, just bring me some water. (MARCUS *looks at* IAIN *again and waves him to the desk.* IAIN *gets up calmly and walks over.*) Hi, Robbo. Grab a seat.

IAIN: (*Sitting.*) *You* look like Atlas.

MARCUS: Atlas?

IAIN: You know, the weight of the world, etc.

[ABBY *places a plastic cup of water gently in front of* MARCUS. MARCUS *downs a few aspirins.*]

MARCUS: You sure you want this job?

IAIN: You tell me.

(MARCUS *picks up the fax on his desk and smacks it with his hand.*)

DIALOGUES

MARCUS: The shit really hit the fan in America last week. Noel left the band. Pissed off completely without so much as leaving a clue. Luckily, Tim Abbot tracked him down. Fuck, it was tense enough already.

IAIN: I heard it was going well for them in the States.

MARCUS: It was! It was fucking brilliant! They came into LA on a wave of expectation, the whole industry excited and talking about them. One of the most important shows of their career, the Whisky, and they fucked it up in front of everyone! No wonder Noel's had it.

IAIN: So, what happened?

MARCUS: Every fucking fucker, in the fucking band and crew, had been up for two days and nights solid doing coke or crystal meth, right up to showtime . . . apart from Noel: he, at least, gave himself a rest on the day of the show. The rest: fucking eyes out on stalks!

ABBY: Line for you on call . . . sorry, that's call for you on line one.

MARCUS: Don't talk to me about lines. Whoever it is, I'll call them back . . . where was I?

IAIN: Fucking eyes out on stalks.

MARCUS: Noel had to not only watch, but be a party to his songs being ripped to shreds by his band. I had a bust up with the guys . . . they had a bust up with themselves and Noel took the entire tour float and buggered off.

IAIN: And the vibe now?

MARCUS: I want to say back on track, but it's four wheels on a very dodgy wagon.

IAIN: Isn't that the way it always is, with any band?

MARCUS: I suppose. (MARCUS *smiles, crushes the fax in his hand and throws it into a wastepaper bin.*) Yeah, I suppose it is. They went straight from Japan where they were treated like stars to the American club circuit, living out of one another's pockets, band and crew on the same bus; it's a tough transition to make.

IAIN: Boulevard of Broken Dreams and all that.

MARCUS: Are you on drugs?

IAIN: (*Smiling.*) What do you want from me?

MARCUS: I want to stretch your initial security brief: I want you to road manage the band as well. When they get back into Europe, I want it to be fun again – they need that if they're to stay together. I want to make things more comfortable, give them a taste of where the hard work is taking them.

ABBY: Call for you on line two. Will you take it?

(MARCUS *shoots* ABBY *a look as if to say, 'What do you think?'*)

MARCUS: You'll handle all the logistics through to Christmas.

IAIN: Jingle all the way.

MARCUS: I'm not saying it's going to be easy.

IAIN: Give me some clues about budget and I'll start the ball rolling.

MARCUS: Talk to Alex about budgets, Europe's going to be great – trust me.

IAIN: Didn't the Devil say that to someone once?

MARCUS: It's gonna be great. (MARCUS *casts his eye over the silver and gold discs which no one has had time to hang.*) It's just, fucking, America.

CHAPTER 6

HEY, DROOGY, DON'T CRASH HERE

Even on the road to damnation a man must rest his foot somewhere.
MADMEN AND SPECIALISTS, WOLE SOYINKA

BEFORE THE BAND FLEW TO JAPAN, they held up one more hoop for me to leap through – a different-coloured fish altogether. In a homecoming of sorts, Oasis provided me with my very first direct experience of their cultural roots: Manchester and the legendary Hacienda club. There is a treadmill routine to life on the road and Oasis are comfortably into that groove, but in Manchester all stay at home in the bosom of family, except Noel.

* * *

Noel and I are cruising past the Brittannia Hotel — Noel Coward-meets-Happy Eater – in another dented minicab on the way to another soundcheck. As good a time as any to talk. I'm wondering why Noel doesn't live here anymore. 'Do these streets feel like home to you?' Noel looks at me, then gazes out of the cab window without answering. 'Just wondering.'

'There's a lot of hurt for me here.' Noel keeps his gaze out of the window. 'A girl.' He turns and looks at me.

'A girl?'

'A girl; a very intense relationship.' He puts his hand inside his pocket as if looking for something, but pulls out nothing. 'I was on the road with the Inspirals. I knew then that I wanted another kind of life, that I could never make the relationship work. It still hurts like hell. I don't care to stay here.'

*   *   *

In the back of that anonymous car, I saw for the first time the essential emptiness that Noel carries. If honest, most of us would admit to its presence from time to time. But the songwriter knows exactly where it's kept and it's from here that he tells his stories. The darkness I saw then I would see again and again. Liam also has it. I never felt it in the other members of the band. I don't say that the brothers carry clouds of despondency with them – they are as quick to laughter as any – but the sadness is palpable and, if anything, it is this that gives depth. Imagine a potter's wheel: as the clay spins carelessly, the potter reaches to impose his will upon it. As he pulls the shapeless material into ordered form, it is necessary to force the perimeters in order that this new chalice should have the capacity to fill its purpose – to hold, to contain. These perimeters must be stretched and stretched again, even to the point of breaking. The more pressure the naked clay resists, the greater its potential. In the same way, whatever doesn't kill us makes us stronger. This is the depth, born of pressure, that the brothers demonstrate. However far they fly from Manchester, and however much they protest otherwise, their fractured past is only a few steps behind. 'Money can't buy me love.'

But there were nights when the past would catch up. With Liam particularly. A late night in Tokyo and Liam and I sat well into the early hours. In the normal way of things, both Gallagher brothers keep 'mum' but, on this occasion, I could feel that Liam wanted to talk something out, needed an audience. It was me, and I listened.

So much is made, and has been catalogued, of Liam's ability to play the role of 'pop star'. In the industry, and especially on the road, the term pop star is intended as a slight: an expression that you spit out to describe the very worst kind of petulant and childish behaviour. And yes, Liam is more than expert at reminding you that it is his ball and, consequently, his rules will apply. As he struggled to find the right words, I got the impression that he, as well as I, was listening to them for the first time. Noel had previously told me that Liam's biggest problem was his being spoiled as a way of life – in fact, the only way of life he had ever known.

There are, of course, three Gallagher brothers, and it would not be unreasonable to expect behavioural similarities as well as the undeniable physiological traits they share. There aren't any. Noel, Liam and Paul seem to share only eyebrow and accent, as if from some point in their shared past they had each set off determinedly in different directions, targeting very different futures. My own feeling is that they were thrown into those personal and solitary trajectories by events, or by an event – the loss of a father.

Mine got the good news when I was twelve, and I went right off track. My dad died; Tommy Gallagher left the family home in 1985. Stop and think about it: how would you feel? Both Noel and Liam had confided to me that there was no possible way back into their hearts for the man who – as far as they were concerned – was designated ex-father, ex-role model, ex-family head. Ex-pect no sympathy, ex-pect no quarter.

For him to turn up after the band's show unannounced in the bar of the Westbury Hotel in Dublin, in March 1996, can only be filed under blind optimism. According to the national papers, Liam and Tommy ended up brawling on the floor. I shouldn't think anyone was overly surprised by this.

There is weirdness between the three Gallagher juniors too. I still can't get my head around having to sneak backstage passes to elder brother Paul, at thirty years old a grown man, on the first night of the Irvine Beach shows in Scotland, July 1995, in defiance of management policy, which ultimately derives from the Noel/Liam axis. Why wouldn't you want your brother to share your success? Having Paul Gallagher crying his eyes out on my shoulder when I dug him from the grave that is the 'not quite' VIP bar is not somewhere I want to be again.

Liam agreed with Noel that he had been spoiled and continued that, in the absence of a father, or a father figure, there had been no one to stop him indulging himself in whatever took his fancy. There were, he said, other men who came and tried to fill the old man's boots, but none he could respect and, ultimately, they all came up short against Mrs Gallagher's expectations. With people I have never met, but have talked to or have heard talked of, I find they fall into two camps when you finally make their acquaintance. Either they look nothing at all like you had imagined they would, or they are identical to the images in your mind's eye. Peggy Gallagher is exactly how I'd pictured her from Noel and Liam's occasional comments: immaculately turned out, matronly, firm-backed and looking you straight in the eye at all times. I met her on several occasions, always when her boys were about to put on a show, and in her eyes you could see pride and nerves in equal measure on the 'lads'' behalf. A real mam.

I believe that, when their biological father left, Noel looked to himself for guidance and Liam turned to apron strings. Paul Gallagher, older and a little more fully formed, was a 'lad' and is a 'lad'. One thing is sure: they were brought up knowing the difference between right and wrong. Liam might act as if he has no intention of growing up, but his worst moments are almost always echoed by profound apology. His mother's voice and Irish Catholic no-nonsense view of morality pinches at his conscience, and prods him when he behaves like a Grade-A Dickhead. These apologies take at least a week to emerge – begrudgingly – from a bashfully grumpy Liam. Although he'll never allow public access to his conscience, they at least surface, albeit in private. No other 'pop star' I've ever dealt with even bothers.

Liam achieved three personal insights that night in Tokyo: that a proper father would have been cool; that, yes, he had been spoiled; and that his mother, above all else and everyone, is his lighthouse. More importantly, in that sterile Japanese hotel room, he let his guard drop and showed a dignity that I hope is still with him. A week later in Osaka, I tried to capture on film something of his loneliness. He was leaning against a fourth-storey window looking out, the city sprawled around him, another uncared-for drink effortlessly balanced in hand. His stance echoed the classic image of Sammy Davis Junior, similarly positioned forty years earlier in New York (and reprised by The Pogues for the cover of their 1987 Christmas single 'Fairytale of New York') – and, similarly, alone.

* * *

Noel and I join the rest of the band inside the Hacienda. Outside there is a glimpse of the future – a string of excited fans surround the building begging anyone with a tour pass for a space on the guest-list, which is already six hundred per cent full with 'guests' still filtering in. Evan Dando lurches into the club, and sadly the bitterest of Lemonheads is playing that well-known rock 'n' roll party game. Can you see a thing? C'mon down, cries the gamesmaster. Mr Dando, you are our next contestant, what can you see? Laydeez and gennelmen, he can't see a thing. He flits between the concrete interior of the Hacienda and wherever the hell he is today. See you later, Evan. Sure, you're on the list. Hope you enjoy the show. Good luck. Bez from the Happy Mondays is our next celebrity contestant. Like Phil, our backline tech, he is gaunt and angular, abstract in movement.

'Just dropping by to wish the band well.'

Thanks, Bez. Next.

It's a wild-arsed night. Before the show, minutes before the show, ex-Mondays singer Shaun Ryder is in the dressing room and he wants to stand by the side of the stage and watch. I screw my diplomatic head firmly in place as Phil leads me to him.

'This is Shaun Ryder from...'

'Yes, thank you, Phil, I know exactly who he is. Shaun, how can I help you?'

'Listen, you're their man, are you? Nice one. I got my wife with me . . . we really wanna see the show from the stage. Can you sort us?'

At another venue this might be cool, but at the Hac, as Shaun well knows, there is no practical way in which I can accommodate him. 'I'm sorry, Shaun, we just don't have the space.'

'You can do it for me, I know you can.'

'Look, I have to give Jason and Phil room to work. I can put you both in the mixing booth out front.' Front, of course, is what this is all about. The Mondays are a tired skag-ridden memory and Black Grape still a long way in the future. Shaun, once 'ace face' around here, needs to be seen right in the very centre of the new centre of all things rock and, indeed, to paraphrase Q, roll. What I kept from Ryder was the fact that Noel had made it quite clear that he didn't want him up there.

'Do you know who I am, you cunt? I've stood on that stage a thousand times.'

'Yeah, I know who you are.' I'm starting to feel repetitive. 'And respect for the music . . . but I don't have room. The best place to see this is with Coyle out front. You and your wife are welcome there.'

73

'Cunt.'

Come on, Shaun, give me a break.

'I'm an elephant and elephants never forget. My posse's here and you're a dead man. You won't leave Manchester alive.'

Yeah, well, thanks a bunch, Shaun, you're still not going to be on that stage. It's a chilling moment though. Manchester is gangster-run, a crack city; people do get killed. Right here and now, I'm awake to my surroundings, big time.

Showtime and, I swear to God, Oasis are having fun. Everyone is grinning from ear to ear. 'Live Forever' is dedicated to Alan McGee, the Creation Records magnate who, perhaps more than anybody – band excluded – is responsible for putting Oasis on the world's stage.

Beyond the cultivation of hemp [*Cannabis sativa*] for its fibre for making garments and household linens by a large part of the people of northern Europe and Asia, the Arabians cultivated a variety of the wild plant, growing but three to five feet, for the resinous gum, hashish, or bhang or banque, an intoxicating drug. Æschylus also states that it was burned and used for vapour baths, while Herodotus says the Scythians were intoxicated by inhaling the fumes of the burning seed. (Hemp [*Cannabis sativa*], S S Boyce, 1900.)

After the show, the subterranean dressing room is swamped with the band, crew, management, record company and many faces from the past, including Noel's ex. She's breathtaking – Kate Moss's face with Claudia Schiffer's body – a supermodel for the working man. That's got to hurt, Noel. How could you let her go? This rock 'n' roll circus is obviously very important to you. Evan's here, still wasted; Bez, a length behind, closing fast. Shaun 'run you outta town' Ryder holds court in a smoke-filled corner – reefer madness.

The leaf, when dried and smoked, is also said to alleviate pain, producing a narcotic, intoxicating effect, increasing the appetite, and giving rise to mental cheerfulness. When the resinous gum which exudes from the plant is taken internally in small doses it produces hilarity, and the patient soon becomes insensible ... Gunjah is an East Indian word for the dried hemp foliage, which was smoked for its intoxicating effects. The seed is used to feed birds and fowls, and to make oil for paints and for making soap. (As before, S S Boyce, 1900.)

At this point, two muscular 'thunksters' bruise their way through the house security, who have already given up any effort of doing their job properly. (They want to go home. Tell you what, gents, you might as well.) So on come a couple of monied-casual hulks, red blood cells outnumbering neurons.

''Ere y'are, geezer, we're with Shaun Ryder.'

My response is tired. 'It's not Shaun's gig.'

The larger of the two large people doesn't switch on. 'Well, we're gonna be doing security for Oasis from now on.'

'Oasis are already secure with me . . . and will be from now on. I'll tell Mr Ryder you called.' Surprisingly, and thankfully, they file out with no further resistance.

I do get out of Manchester alive . . . this time. I vow that I will never do another gig here without someone to watch my back. Violence, or the potential for violence, is not new to me, obviously, but it's dawning on me that, for Oasis, it is the norm. Manchester is the band's hometown and these are mean streets.

CHAPTER 7

HOW TO GET
ON IN SOCIETY

You taught me language, and my profit on't
Is I know how to curse. . .
THE TEMPEST, WILLIAM SHAKESPEARE

LOOKING BACK AT THE TOUR ITINERARY I had produced
for those first steps with the band, I found in the Notes section
an entry for Day One, 1 November 1994. It read, 'Band to have
dinner with record company in Paris.' Well, yes, sort of.

That these five errant sons of Manchester were in Paris at
all, and being treated like champions by *any* record company,
was down to the plain fact that Noel Gallagher is such a gifted
songwriter. On tour, Noel's room was always the most crowded,
not just with the tangible – items like his Guild acoustic guitar –
but with the many voices clamouring to be songs. Sleep for Noel
was snatched during long journeys from gig to gig. His nights
were spent working and reworking, moulding and refining a new
generation of Oasis material. At this time, these were the voices

that would become the songs that would become *(What's the Story) Morning Glory?* Beneath the morning glory and the wash of alcohol, it was Noel.

The first day in the first real month of winter 1994 had been given over to promotion and, I remember, we had been all over what is sometimes sentimentally called the City of Lovers, accompanied by a melange of journalists, photographers and TV crews. My listing in the itinerary was as Assistant Tour Manager/ Security Co-ordinator – the rules had changed. Oasis Inc. now looked to me to arrange, juggle and assemble completely all the varied elements of road life for them.

This was standard road management, something I had just finished doing for the ill-fated 'supergroup' BBM — Jack Bruce and Ginger Baker of Cream fame, and Gary Moore of Thin Lizzy fame. Then I had adopted what I call the 'reactive' method of working, which is finding out what the worthy want, when they want it and, most importantly, making sure they get it. Arse--kissing, if you like. If you are ever fortunate, or unfortunate, enough to find yourself operating in this fashion, be prepared to hurtle around like a blue-arsed fly, from breakfast to sundown, fulfilling the increasingly erratic whims and fancies of band and management.

With Oasis, I decided to be pro-active, to create a plan, a shape for each day and, without being totally inflexible, stick to it. This demanded a leap of faith from everyone. As far as Noel, Liam, Bonehead, Guigsy and Tony were concerned, it represented a serious change in the way they conducted themselves. Bonehead remarked to me, 'We're not used to being told quite so forcibly what's goin' on. But it's good . . . yeah, it's good.' I wasn't entirely sure what he meant by good – I know what I mean by good – and one late night I told Noel that I didn't want to be the band's best mate, that I just wanted to do a good job for them.

It was always very clear whose side I was on. The ubiquitous press soon found this out whenever they sent their over-keen minions to intrude on what, in anybody's book, is private space. Notebooks, microphones, cameras and prying intentions were unceremoniously redirected by me and what was on- or off-record never more clearly defined.

All in all, I would like to think that we finished that first full day of the tour with a mutual respect. I watched Oasis perform unpleasant tasks patiently, professionally, and with good humour: they saw that absolutely no one would find it easy to get past me or be allowed to take the piss. So, after a sensible working day, it was time for a hard day's night with more record-label credit cards than you could shake a stick at. Marcus was there, and he had a card; Michel was there too, he had a card; Tim Abbot was also there, and he had a card; Jeremy Pearce . . . total, four . . . because he had a card. Enough flexible friends for the evening.

Tim Abbot was one of the key players at Creation Records. Tim was very close to Noel and, indeed, to the band as a whole. He was the one who, when Noel vanished in the States, was able to convince him not to give up on Oasis. Tim operated on a kind of freelance basis as an ideas man for the band; he played an important role in the communication between band and media. Aside from this, he was a very cool guy to have around for morale and, on the road, this is a valuable service to be able to provide, as essential a purpose as any other provided by the crew – a kind of ambiance technician.

Jeremy Pearce was another good guy, and a fan. A lawyer by profession, Jeremy had been around the block, his first job in the 'biz' being bailing out Ike Turner from a Class-A drugs-possession charge. Perhaps fortuitously, he was now working with Oasis. He was the label's big shot, a guv'nor. Across the board there is always a bottom line. Jeremy was the one who decided what that bottom line was: how much could be spent, when it could be spent and on what it could be spent. Jeremy, as befitting one so important, had a splendid selection of credit cards for us to spank.

* * *

The evening starts in a suitably expensive Italian restaurant in Montmartre. Nobody in the band comes from the kind of background that makes a trip to such po-faced quasi-sophistication a comfortable experience. As we sit at a long table in the centre of the room, the surrounding eyes of etiquette, either bulging in starched convention or demi-hooded in distaste at having riff-raff forced upon them, are turned briefly towards us, then down bourgeois noses trying their hardest to be patrician. Clearly, we are regarded as a chimps' tea party in the making. The artificial civility is hilarious.

Our proceedings commence with the record company suggesting aperitifs, perhaps a glass of champagne . . . a splash of Ricard?

'Jack Daniel's and Coke.' Noel.

Guigsy: 'Jack and Coke.'

'Three!' Liam's decided to take it easy.

'Yup.' Tony McCarroll, the current drummer.

'I'll have a bottle of red wine, please.' Ah, Bonehead, you smooth bastard.

Drinks now out of the way, it's time to consider the menu. The linen tablecloth has been starched to reflect the patrons and is laid with a flourish over crumpled denim for that certain *je ne sais quoi*. It is laid by a portly, moustached cartoon Italian waiter: think Disney's *The Lady and the Tramp* and you've got the picture. The food order for the band is a uniform steak and chips. But hold on, Noel is ordering pasta.

Liam shoots a quizzical glance, caterpillar eyebrows raised. Wheels are in motion; you can almost read his mind. 'Poof,' he says curtly, saving us the trouble.

No sport here and we're all wondering what to do while we wait for the nosebags to be strapped on.

'More drinks?' An excellent idea. In no time there are bottles of champagne, and red, white and rose wines (we're covering all bases). However, with the exception of arch-sophisticate Bonehead, Jack and Coke is the blunt instrument of choice for the band.

* * *

When Oasis first began to tour, and I mean in its nascent form in the very, very beginning – on the eighth day God created Oasis . . . who threw a monkey wrench in all his good works – in *those* early days, Bonehead was the tour manager! Even now, when he and Liam travel from Manchester, Bonehead is the name under which the flight tickets are held, much to the consternation of the British Airways rep: 'Err, um, so it's Mr Bonehead, is it?' Yes, it most certainly is. Bonehead is definitely with the programme. Even before Oasis were successful, he owned an elegant Victorian house, knew which saucer to drink from and had developed a taste for red wine, albeit by the vat-load. All the refinements, Bonehead had them. He's a good man, a fine father and, as luck would have it, a watertight rhythm guitarist. Though never adopt the trainspotter approach to guitar playing with him: for example, what strings do you use in April? Bonehead doesn't want to be Jimi Hendrix and gets positively embarrassed if asked to play anything 'widdly widdly' and, besides, Noel wears that hat. After a show in LA in February 1995, some guitar fetishist bluffed his way into the dressing room and began to offer his opinions, completely unsought.

'Man, all you played was, like, A, C, D or G.'

Bonehead's reply could only be construed as helpful. 'Listen, dickhead, that might well be all I played, but I'm the one playing it, I'm the one in the band, and you paid to see me do it.' A fair point.

* * *

The necessary evil of eating is now out of the way and it is time for a change of scene. Where better than Lillie la Tigresse? Tigresse is a trendy strip joint, the kind of place that could really only exist in Paris, a quintessential co-existence of low life and high culture. Roll up, roll up, we got ladies, they are naked and they move. The clientele here always looks good to me, a super-chic eclectic mix, it appears, of gangster, pimp, gangster-pimp, relaxing businessman, and the modish young Parisian. Oh yes, and naked ladies, all beautiful, all dancing on the bar – fabulous. Tigresse also serves the finest margaritas anywhere in Europe. Can't think why we spend so much time here.

We walk into the bar through a swathe of descending red velvet and into a wall of sound. The place is packed and everybody shouts; you have to, not so much to be heard, it's more a question of manners or tradition. Although Bonehead has only been drinking wine instead of joining the others in Tennessee sippin', he has by now drunk a lot of wine. I find myself between him and Tony McCarroll as tequilas start to arrive, courtesy of Michel. (Tony will be allowed to leave the band in the not too distant future, 'musical differences' being cited. But even now, in November 1994, the only member of Oasis who has a civil word for him is Bonehead.) Bonehead is swaying on his stool. Our table is tucked away in a corner, but he still manages in the course of five minutes to spill everybody's drink; that is, everybody's drink in the club, not just 'us' everybody. An optimistic trip to the gents wreaks havoc. Those who see him coming throw their own drinks away to save him the trouble. What the hell, the record company, who bought them all anyway, are now busy apologising and compensating for loss. The traffic from bar to table is unceasing, plastic imprints bartered for booze, and never fast enough. The walls we build to insulate for fear of discovery are coming down and I feel able to ask a question of Tony which has been troubling me.

* * *

When with Oasis, Tony received flak from the rest of the band and crew that was often brutal. He was singled out as the archetypal 'new boy' at school and, short of having his head flushed down a toilet bowl, bore the weight of ridicule. It always started with a questioning of how he played the drums, but very quickly turned to poison and sought to completely annihilate his intelligence and appearance. A selection of his personal traits would be extracted without anaesthetic and slashed to ribbons. He spent most of his time when in the band's company garlanded with aural razor wire. It surprised me how he was able to deal with it.

Budgetary restrictions being what they were, everyone on the road shared a room. Liam and Guigsy were partners and Tony was paired with Bonehead. Noel shared his room with a muse. Bonehead, at least, had the decency to lay off most of the time and even offered support if it looked as if Tony was going under. Noel usually led the attacks, but his problems with Tony were for a different reason than Liam and Guigsy's. Noel had a focused idea of what Oasis should be musically and Tony was becoming less and less a part of that idea. Noel treats his songs like his own family and he was starting to see Tony's drumming as an assault on his children. Tony told me that throughout the constant criticism he was sustained by the knowledge that, despite all of it, he remained the drummer in the greatest rock 'n' roll band in the world. The fact that they couldn't take that away from him enabled him to suffer the hurt he felt each time a blow was dealt, whether personal or musical. Well, it was true for a while, at least.

* * *

Guigsy and I have been discussing sport throughout the evening. Normally not one to say much at all, with a drink or nine, Guigsy loosens up a lot and I am hearing for the first time – and it will not be the last – what a fine sporting talent he possesses. Apparently, his father had played with George Best — Besty to his friends. Guigsy's own footling talents had been encouraged with the aid of some revolutionary training techniques, which apparently involved the young McGuigan being tied to a tree. Having never been a footballer, I am prepared to accept this. Anyway, everybody's conversation has now deteriorated into somewhere way off sensible and shouting has become the norm.

Marcus looks over to Noel and gives me some inside track: 'You can't see his eyes. When he's pissed, they disappear; he's just a smile.' Sure enough, Noel enjoying himself is just that: a grin on legs. We are moving on – we have to. We're in search of the crack one hundred yards away at another bar.

Iced water from champagne buckets is hurled about the room. Guigsy is standing on his chair, demonstrating the perfect square-cut to nobody in particular. The landlord couldn't give a toss: business is booming. There's a svelte waitress wearing a double holster: tequila left; champagne right. We all agree on what's needed – tequila slammers. She's poured us out. A line of hands presses down across the thick rims of slammer glasses. Hope our bottoms are up to it. A crack of glass on wood before the distilled dew of the Mexican agave plant, aroused by the champagne, is sent bubbling and gushing down our throats. A little more mayhem to minds already muddled and mashed.

*　*　*

The main achievement of the evening was that we all got back to the hotel – all of fifty metres away – or so I thought. In the morning, I discovered that Noel was absent without leave.

CHAPTER 8

DAY OF THE DEAD

2nd November, 1755. Earthquake devastates the city of Lisbon.
NEWSPAPER HEADLINE

Dear Diary

2 NOVEMBER 1994

9:30 am   Awake with some difficulty after last night.
                 Am certainly in my room, I think. Who's that
                 in the other bed? It's Bod, the senior Gallagher
                 brother. I dimly remember him crashing out
                 there at 6:00 am. Must pull myself together,
                 start waking the band and crew. Due to leave at
                 11:00 am.

10:00 am   I find Marcus ahead of me. But he went to sleep
                 yesterday.

11:30 am   We are ready to leave. There is a small fly in the ointment: the absence of Noel. I send the bus off with almost a complete party. Must find the missing person. Luckily, I took the precaution of logging the phone numbers of the last ladies he was consorting with at 4:00 am. If I don't find him, I'm fucked.

12 noon   I've made a phone call. A contrite female voice has confirmed that they did abduct the songwriter. He's pushing a few 'z's, happily unaware that he's missed the bus – a solo artist now.

12:15 pm   Taxi!

1:00 pm   'How the fuck did you know I was here?' I've impressed Noel. I give the impression that I am all-seeing and hide the fact of how bereft of ideas I would have been had he not been there.

3:00 pm   We have both looked and felt better as we board the train for Lille. Conversation is limited. We drink the train dry of sweet, fizzy, rehydrating Coke – breakfast of champions.

4:30 pm   The train arrives at Lille. We hail a cab and head for the venue. Traffic is appalling. Unbelievably, we pass the tour bus.

4:45 pm   I stop the cab, wake Noel. In pouring rain, we run through the snarl of vehicles and wave down the bus. It's Marie Celeste aboard, everyone asleep in the back.

5:10 pm   Just minutes from the venue. Dazed band and crew wake from slumber in ones and twos. No one can quite believe Noel and I are sitting on the bus. Bonehead is first to express himself. "E'y'are, you fuckers weren't on this bus when it left Paris. How'd you manage that?' We let them all mull it over without offering an explanation.

5:20 pm   The venue is a faceless concrete building under a flyover. It is still raining.

5:25 pm   Common to this type of venue, there is a lack of windows. Everything inside is uniform grey under inadequate lights.

5:30 pm   Dressing room is a minor improvement, finished in manic orange – tangoed again. Where are the style police when you need them?

6:30 pm   Soundcheck is uneventful.

7:45 pm   Into a press schedule. Journalists from the 'we're at least as cool as the band' school of journalism. Calibre of question is particularly poor. I wrap the whole sorry affair up after fifteen minutes.

8:00 pm   Time to kill. Bonehead amuses us by trying on my jacket and waterproof hat. Being substantially smaller, he is lost, the hat slipping down over his nose – the final scene from the movie *Big*.

8:30 pm   Support band, Echobelly, begin their set. Oasis pay no attention.

9:30 pm   Ticket sales are a little less than one hundred per cent. Oasis deliver an assured show, but without their customary edge.

10:45 pm   We don't hang around. Straight back to the hotel.

11:10 pm   No call for partying tonight. A dingy Chinese take-away serves a purpose for the night.

12:30 am   Everyone slipping away to bedrooms. A quiet night as the rain slaps against the windows, and the wet streets and an early bed bring heroes and fans back to reality – on the same level.

1:30 am   I walk a corridor to my room. I think I hear
            Liam talking in his sleep, but I can't be sure.

CHAPTER 9

DOWN AND OUT IN LYON AND LONDON

*...his heart shook within the cage of his breast as he
tasted the rumour of that storm.*
Ulysses, James Joyce

THE FRENCH PROMOTER, Dominique Revert, has organised a party, or so he says, for the band at a Bohemian club situated in the old town, the misshapen quarter of Lyon. We make our way through a maze of skinny cobbled streets; history shivers, ill-lit in the resolute rain and with just a trace of fog suspended in the half-light. It is decidedly more Hunch Back than Gene Kelly. We are three taxis curling along the hushed and ancient passages.

With a collective sigh of relief, the cabbies dump us on the incongruous period set and leave rapidly. There is an old stench in the air. We approach a gnarled and grimy building that corresponds with the address Dominique has scrawled for us across the back of a tatty set list.

It is taken for granted that one of the perks of being the next big thing is automatic entry, and VIP treatment in any den in the belly of iniquity. Given that we think our arrival is keenly anticipated, the brusque knockback we receive at the door goes down like a knackered lift. The surly gatekeeper is not well versed in social niceties but, luckily, over the years, I have developed an easy familiarity with these high-level and delicate negotiations. We're in. We are now verbally accosted by the owner of the club. He has never heard of Oasis; he has heard of Dominique Revert, but doesn't see what it has to do with him. Another round of diplomatic talks and the outcome provides us with a table in a peculiar corner of the establishment, perched above a rickety flight of stairs. The band settle in, but are subdued. Drinks are ordered.

'And 'ow you pay for zese drinks?' A waiter, as smug as a wide-mouthed frog on a heated lily pad, props his order book in his belt.

Just when I thought I'd finished with the Henry Kissinger bit, more gentle persuasion is needed. 'Isn't it customary to expect a small degree of hospitality to be extended to invited guests?' Surely a reasonable reply?

A bottle of Ballantine whisky, accompanied by Coke, ice and a few beers, is begrudgingly thrown at us. Still, it's not a disagreeable place, more a late-night drinking retreat than a club, with music at a corresponding level, in harmony, rather than in competition, with conversation. One or two faces – the more gregarious of the otherwise aloof French late-nighters – sidle up and attach themselves to what is, to them, a curious gang. An overly earnest, half-bright and misguided student of the BritPop phenomenon tricks Liam into conversation with an opening gambit that is all compliment. Somehow, the exchange turns off the safer highway of flattery and, through a grave map-reading error, turns sharply into oncoming traffic. Henri Misinformed is grinding up the gears with neither clutch nor sense and rams the chat into matters of Gallagher family history. We all hear Liam's voice edging inexorably towards aggression.

My attention is diverted from Guigsy's riveting monologue (he is once again being roped tightly to Manchester's limited selection of shrubbery by George Best). Clearly unaware of the concept of *entente cordiale*, Henri has inadvertently managed to insult Peggy Gallagher, Liam and Noel's main. The shit is about to hit the fan.

''Ere y'are, 'ere y'are, dick, what's me fuckin' mam to you?' Liam's blue touch paper has been lit.

Retiring is not an option and I move in between the warring factions. Quite frankly, I'm tired with the way this evening has turned out. I pick up the Frenchman by the scruff of his neck and bundle him towards the foot-weary staircase. Liam rises to follow, continuing the heated exchange.

'Fucking French dickhead.'

Liam's antagonist remains spirited and determined but, even in a one-on-one situation, he probably couldn't handle Liam. He is slight, bookish, bespectacled; there is nothing in his bookishness of the casual, elegant Bohemia that characterises the Parisian *étudiant*. Frankly, he is a geek, but a feisty geek.

'What iz eet you so are arrogant?' Well, that should do it. 'Who iz eet ah cannot spiek with 'im? Fuck off, you. Fuck off, all of you.' Other assorted pidgin opinions are loudly voiced, brought about by a pressing need to trade insults.

I now hold him at the top of the stairs and slowly begin the boring process of prising his fingers from the banisters and getting him down and out of harm's, and everybody else's, way. We progress in an ungainly fashion, like Siamese twins arguing with their own single-motor system. Just as I am thinking that a successful and painless removal is on the horizon, Liam plays his joker. Leaning over the wooden handrail above us, which is as flimsy as balsa wood, he begins to rain punches on his opponent's unprotected head, three to the temple, two just for fun. Alone and outnumbered, Henri is finally disheartened and becomes dead weight in my hands. In the short time from this moment to his inelegant departure, his eye is already closing behind an ugly and rapidly inflating purple-yellow cheekbone. I would feel sorry for him, but insulting someone's mother is not the best method of endearment in my book of *How To Win Friends and Influence People*.

I return to the others, back up those bloody stairs again. I now have a thoroughly unpleasant taste in my mouth. I look across at Liam; he looks as sick from the last five minutes as I am. Clearly, there is no way we are going to salvage the night. On an unspoken cue, we all get up and trail out in silence. It is a moment stripped of all glamour, all illusion; the echo of a human condition that cannot escape misunderstanding.

*   *   *

Monday, 7 November 1994, Air France flight no. AF3570, Marseilles to London. Check in 12:10 pm., depart 13:10 pm., arrive London

Heathrow 14:10 pm. (all timings local). Wednesday, 9 November 1994, the Q Awards to mark the publication's hundredth issue. Park Lane Hotel, Piccadilly, London.

As we spilled with our laughter through and across the fabricated panels and moving corridors of Heathrow, ambling in good humour to the baggage-claim carousel, we discussed the approaching awards. Liam, vehemently anti-London and, at that point, anti-industry back-slapping, was heading back to Manchester. Bonehead, with a baby on the way, was to do likewise, as was Tony, who wasn't interested in any of it. Guigsy had some athletic and imaginative sex to be getting on with; a new and exciting girlfriend was waiting for him and promises had been made. Noel, then, was to be the sole representative for Oasis.

* * *

As we bimble through the airport, Noel turns and asks me if I would like to come along to the awards for the ride.

Don't be stupid, Noel, I've got some trainspotting to do.

It is agreed, signed, sealed and delivered. Noel and I will meet at the band's management offices on the Wednesday and have us some fun.

Oasis are not short of nominations: Best Live Act; Best Album; Best New Act. Noel, in his inimitable way, is realistic in his expectations. 'Basically, Robbo, we deserve to win everything, but Best New Act is mine today; next year I'll have the lot.'

Gipsy Noel has spread the tarot and caressed the crystal. This fortune-telling will be very telling.

Noel and I are tucked into an ordinary minicab with a girl of the moment, Rebecca de Ruva. We cruise away from Wyndham Place and head for the Park Lane Hotel. Foremost in Noel's mind is a suitably unambiguous acceptance speech.

I suggest he just keeps it short: 'I applaud your wisdom, thanks.'

'Nice one, geezer. Consider that nicked.'

An honour, indeed. So now I'm going to be up there with Marc Bolan and the Beatles.

As we approach the velvet crush outside the entrance to the ballroom where the ceremony will take place, I think it best to sidestep the TV crews and paparazzi jackals. The driver stretches the car laterally to the kerb, twenty yards away from the reception committee. His dexterous manoeuvre suggests a car built in Toon Town and lessons from Roger Rabbit. We enter, unmarked, through the hotel's main entrance, brushing past the ornate mirrored double doors.

We are seated at a table close to the toilets – ideal placing. All the tables are circular, each surrounded by hopeful artists and their supporting players. Most are smiling above knotted stomachs; stakes are high for those who care about industry recognition; for those who don't, it's a damn good jolly-up. The Creation/Oasis table is leaning heavily towards not taking any of it too seriously. Dick Green is the Managing Director of Creation Records, and a Benny Hill lookalike to boot. By giving the drinks waiters a substantial tip in advance, he ensures that, whoever wins an award this afternoon, it certainly isn't going to be for sobriety. As awards ceremonies go, the Q thing is an unpretentious, straightforward affair: a few speeches; review of the year; the awards themselves;

lunch; and, finally, carriages home. However, the awards of 1994 are to feature something of a curve-ball – one of the guest speakers is Tony Blair.

Tony Blair is, at this point, Leader of the Labour Party in opposition to John Major's Conservative Party, which, in turn, is in opposition to the prosperous future of our once great nation. All indicators suggest that Blair is the British Prime Minister in waiting, one general election away from guiding the United Kingdom into the next millennium. We can kid ourselves about rock 'n' roll's power to change lives, save souls, etc., etc., *ad infinitum*. But here is a man who might wield real power – the kind that corrupts, absolutely. As guest speaker, he links any number of insipid, vapid platitudes together and passes them off as a speech. It sounds as if he wrote it in the back of the ministerial vehicle that continually ferries him from one fairground to another. Nevertheless, he receives a rapturous and 'heart-warming' reception from the 'biz'. All are keen to show their caring, sharing hearts on designer sleeves. At a guess, at least sixty per cent of the chosen few in the room today probably voted Tory last time in 1992 and will, no doubt, do so again: I'm all right, Jack, pull the ladder up. Still, Blair is enjoying himself.

I enjoyed myself too, and so did Noel. In the prize-giving ceremony, he duly picked up Best New Act on behalf of Oasis. As promised, he stole my words for his thank-you speech; he was welcome to them. Typical of these events, any form starts to fall apart once the gongs have gone, and lots of hugging and kissing begins: loved the record; great timpani on track four, and the bongos, well! At our table near the toilet, we kept ourselves to ourselves and concentrated on getting through the assorted throat-charmers.

Noel signals that a journey to the loo is needed and that I should ride shotgun. Is there ever a safe place to do coke, apart from the unglamorous offices known as the bog? We snake away from the table, queue up and finally take possession of a cubicle. Noel pulls out a white parcel and chops out the narcotic grain on top of an enamel flushing tank. After the pep, we race back to our seats, but not before an unexpected meeting of great minds. Rounding a corner, we bump into the man of red destiny himself, Tony Blair, going through the motions of a sneaky exit stage left. He is accompanied by Mark Ellen, the founding editor of our august hosts, *Q*.

Noel turns to me. 'Robbo, follow me.' A wide smile like the sliver of a waxing moon arches up and tickles both his ears.

Noel's had a hooterful of hooter and he can't resist a chinwag. He's seen off forty quid's worth of Charlie in one swift sweep. This is just beginning to operate his tongue, obviating him of the need to include his brain in the exchange. The future British Prime Minister is a sitting duck.

Mark Ellen is a little more clued-up than Blair with the social hobbies of young Gallagher and his like and makes an attempt to steer his old mate to safety. But, like a veteran pugilist, Noel cuts off all escape routes, leaving Blair with his back against the ropes. 'All right, geezer, nice one.' And with this, Noel thrusts his hand into that of the Labour Party Leader.

Ellen pastes a false and crooked smile bravely in place and

steps into the breach. 'Ah, Tony, this is Noel Gallagher . . . from the group, Oasis.'

Blair, even more familiar with artifice, is one step ahead and has already pulled his happy face from the bag. He enthusiastically pumps Noel's hand. If Noel were a baby, I have no doubt that he would bounce him on his knee. 'Err, Noel Gallagher. Yes, very good.' Noel isn't in the mood to offer advice on either home or foreign policy. 'Lots of luck, mate. Win it for the people.'

Mark Ellen is visibly relieved as Noel and I walk on and the future Prime Minister of England is none the worse for wear.

* * *

The tour resumed one week later in London when the band regrouped for a session with Gered Mankowitz, an A-List photographer whose many credits include the classic Stones shot used for the cover of *Between the Buttons*. Mankowitz was very keen to duplicate this, one of his favourite pictures, this time using Oasis. He assembled the band in exactly the same position on Hampstead Heath as he had the original 'bad lads' almost thirty years previously. Our schedule was particularly tight that day, as we had a flight to catch to Scandinavia. So, while the band sucked in cheeks and flirted with Gered's camera, I went to pack Noel's suitcase. He had neglected to include this on his list of things to do that morning, probably because he had neglected to go to sleep the night before, having spent it with Paul Weller and Jack Daniel's.

Noel was effectively homeless at this time. Although Johnny Marr was to let him have the use of his central-London apartment, Noel, for now, was at home at the Regent Hotel in Marylebone Road – no hardship. The Regent (now called the Landmark) was, and is, one of the finest hotels the city has to offer.

*　*　*

As I let myself into Noel's suite, I cannot help but admire his handiwork. There is no sign of a maid's tidy touch and I wonder whether one has even been allowed in during his entire occupancy. It is one seriously worked-over interior. I don't know when the bomb went off in Noel's suitcase; he had looked unscathed earlier when he turned up to present his best profile. Clothes are everywhere. Perhaps this is a new art form being explored. The debris is too comprehensive to be the product of accident. I decide I like it. Very Picasso: Noel has caught the Guernica dynamic perfectly.

Where to begin? The room contains an entire way of life, and it isn't all coming to Stockholm. I start to sift through the dozen or so empty champagne bottles and numerous empty shells of bourbon, vodka and gin; there might be something he needs among the consumed and discarded. I find some cocaine wraps licked clean, although there are a few traces here and there. My tongue has too much fur on it today, so I pick up the wraps and make a little bonfire with them in a crystal ashtray – just in case. Noel's going to have to wear something, and perhaps would like some of the CDs, books and presents that litter the tables and cabinets. I grab some shoes: there are plenty to chose from – Imelda Marcos would be proud of you, Noel. I avoid any socks and underwear that have seen action.

One of the first signs of a man accumulating money is his rack of freshly dry-cleaned shirts and extravagant boxes of laundered smalls, all hand finished. It is remarkable to see the care that has gone into folding Noel's boxers, most likely by some poor sap working below minimum wage in the bowels of the hotel. In a joint like the Regent, this amount of dry-cleaning and hand-finished laundering will cost you at least £300.00. A few washes and dries in the corner laundrette will come to under a tenner. But why be wishy-washy with your splashy-splashy when there's plenty of loot in the kitty. Between pissing it up and racking it out, it is clear that Noel has had time to go shopping. With so much apparel, it is hard to pin down his wardrobe for this next leg of the tour. As his dresser, I decide, very profoundly, that what I don't pack, he can't wear. Could have some fun with this.

'Abby, it's Robbo, can you do me a favour?' Abby is the lithe and lovely assistant to Marcus, and a cornerstone to all things Oasis.

'Hi, Robbo. Yes, try me.'

'Would you mind nipping out and buying a suitcase?'

'A suitcase?'

'I'm at Noel's hotel, trying to get some things together for him, but I've got more stuff than I can pack.'

'Sure, Robbo.'

So, Abby agrees to nip out and purchase a button-bright new

suitcase and to hightail it over to the Regent so we can pack what's left over.

With this out of the way, all that's left for me is to sort out the hotel bill. Bed and breakfast will be paid by the travel agent, but I will settle the hotel extras – that area in rock 'n' roll so grey it makes Man City FC look colourful. Extras, in essence, will be room service, phone calls and bar bills. Noel has managed £2,500, and there is bugger-all under 'room service' or 'telephone'. It's a treat to be alive.

* * *

We flew to somewhere else, and then we drove to another place – I can't remember where. Let me twist the chronology a little, if I may.

We were rolling out of France in the tour bus, with one of the biggest of all the European music festivals under the band's belt. They came, they saw, etc. Liam has had a little of this and a little of that. The bus is moving – fast. And, suddenly, Liam is dancing on top of the world, on top of the bus: wrapped in a Union Jack, he is 'bus surfing'.

Like I say, we're moving fast. Power lines hang over the road and, as we approach them, Liam is dancing, and singing, and shouting. I worm my head out of the front skylight in the ceiling and plead, 'Liam, come back inside.'

The first electric cable is about to pass above us, and I'm convinced that the young Gallagher will become toast. But suddenly Liam drops flat and shivers of death hush silently over him. Then he leaps back up and, with me in sustained begging mode, repeats the exercise a further four or five times before rejoining us. Captain fucking Scarlet.

* * *

Ah, yes, Cologne, spelled Köln by our German neighbours, and to the Luxor Club. The Luxor Club (or was it the Luxor Bar?) was a pencil-thin dive. It seemed to work back-to-front: toilet-cum-dressing room; one small stage; two bars. Our German promoter was not a man who learned anything quickly. Since the incident in Newcastle where Noel received a black eye, a barrier provision had been written into the band's contract. Not only does a barrier protect the band from a riotous audience, it also protects the audience from itself. For example, if you're in the front row and ailing, then this barrier gives someone, usually me, the space to pluck you out and save your arse. That, primarily, is why they're used, and not as some alienating prerequisite for a bunch of freshly minted prima donnas. These merits explained, the promoter nevertheless ignored our barrier requests throughout Germany. Berlin was madness, Hamburg little better, yet still he maintained that Köln would be different. Jason and Phil had worked their nuts off trying to fashion a substitute out of flight cases and self-locking webbing straps, but it really didn't inspire confidence. The Luxor Club was jammed with heaving bodies. We had a *Blue Peter* construction without the luxury of falling back on one we'd prepared earlier. The barrier was showing signs of wear even before the band left the backstage area. Before going to work that night, I had a serious chat with the guys.

'When the barrier fails . . . and it will . . . when it fails, then expect me to emerge centre stage.'

'Captain Hurricane to the rescue!' Someone in the background makes a joke.

'No "It's only rock 'n' roll" heroics; get off the stage, let the crew fix it, if possible. If not, take the money and run. We can chew the promoter's bollocks off later.'

My itinerary says that the club has a capacity of 500. The crowd is redefining that capacity. In addition, the doors have been left open and a sizeable mob adds weight to the press from outside the building.

I look at my watch and it's 21:45. There is movement on stage. Noel straps on Johnny Marr's Les Paul and bends chords out and into shape as he casts 'Rock 'n' Roll Star' like raw meat. I glance over at the makeshift barrier and it is clear we are in for an early bath.

The barrier doesn't even have the decency to bend. It ups and breaks. Those at the front, always, always, always the weakest, break with it. I signal to Noel. The music stops and Oasis leave the stage. Suddenly, it is mayhem. People at the back immediately push with greater urgency, trying to come forward to see what they're missing, unaware that people at the front have nowhere to go and are in danger of losing slightly more than their composure. Not good. Jason and I invent an agitated sign language on the spot and a mime that would have Marcel eating his heart out. Finally, we bring the crowd to some kind of equipoise and affect some running repairs. The result is not something Isambard Kingdom Brunel, designer of the Clifton Suspension Bridge, would, were he alive, put his hand up to. Anyway, the bugger holds through, but I know damn well that, if such mayhem rules here in Germany, a territory where the band are still relatively unknown, England and the rest of the projected tour is going to be stone bonkers.

CHAPTER 10

SACKER OF CITIES

The Assyrlain came down like the wolf on the fold
And his cohorts were gleaming in purple and gold
'THE DESTRUCTION OF THE SENNACHERIB', LORD BYRON

I HATE TO HAVE TO SAY THIS, but Oasis are not, in any sense, a group. There is no kind of common purpose, philosophy or aim artistically: they're out there, a band of individuals flying solo. It's a condition that most successful bands arrive at eventually, as newfound wealth and exposure to a wider world open windows of opportunity in what were once narrower minds. The Three Musketeers mental-set of 'all for one and one for all' is gradually eroded and replaced by more personal visions and aspirations. Usually, the process takes a while. For example, Lennon and McCartney pulling apart the Beatles; later, Sting disappearing up his own *kundalini* and dispersing the Police; and, more recently, Take That discovering that you can't be a 'lad' forever.

Despite this, Oasis seldom deliver anything under par and this is mainly because you would have to walk a long and crooked mile to find bigger fans of Noel Gallagher's genius than the 'other four'. However, no one else has any creative input as far as the songwriting is concerned, although Liam is able to exert some influence on how the music presents itself. But, all said, they love to play Noel's songs, and this is how Oasis material is viewed by Oasis. What you get for your money is not a group, as such, but a selection of Noel Gallagher tunes written for the Oasis Corporation.

It is Noel's vision that sustains them and, without him, the band's success would be inconceivable. They would sink without trace, Liam's undeniable charisma unable to support them on its own. If Noel ever chose not to write for Liam, there are only two other people whose songs the singer would want to sing: his own and John Lennon's. But Lennon is unavailable and Liam has never shown any concrete sign of having a comparable creative ability to Noel. In a *Sunday Times* interview in February 1996, he tried to convince the journalist that 'I can write better music than our Kid . . . I'm too busy getting off my head.' Maybe. Time will either back that up or bury it. Time's up.

As our coach rolled off a cross-channel ferry to begin the British leg of the tour, that's pretty much how the stage was set: Noel's confidence was through the roof and the gap between them all was widening appreciably.

To a band like Oasis, an overnight ferry crossing is a wonderful opportunity for a jolly-up. Despite the ferry being rocked by an angry sea – the type worse things happen at – we were coming home to great expectations and both the band's and P&O's spirits were fuel enough to steady the boat.

* * *

We have been back in Blighty all of five minutes when, pulling into the first available petrol station, we find our way blocked by a battered Volkswagen Passat, clearly done with its pit-stop. The passengers inside, for some reason, refuse to start up and drive out. A certain unique breed of driver is usually par for the course on a rock 'n' roll tour: never backward in coming forward. Our driver, Steve, is no exception. He waits patiently for two seconds and then blasts the intercontinental coach-sized air horn for slightly more than two seconds. The Passat doesn't move and it is blatantly obvious that another course of action is needed. Steve is the very chap. He leaps from his cab and storms towards the car like a career *apparatchik* finding 007's Aston in Brezhnev's parking space outside the Kremlin at the height of the Cold War. Those in the car decide to adopt an equally provocative attitude and pile out to meet him. There are more robust human specimens than our coach driver and, sure enough, the three who now stand facing Steve are. I think that, perhaps, it's a good time for me to leave the bus and intervene, to see if there isn't some way common sense can triumph here.

Having relegated Steve to the role of Chief Shouter of Abuse, I have a look at the enemy and make three battlefield assessments:

1. They are very drunk
2. They have been drinking a lot
3. Did I mention the drunk thing?

This is all in my favour. It allows me to pursue the option found in *The Bumper Book of Fighting* under the chapter entitled 'Cheating'.

'Gentlemen, you are all drunk. If you don't move the car, I will call the police. And one of you sorry scumbags is clearly designated driver.' Behind me, the level of abuse is developing a choral quality. Having delivered myself of my calculated and manly challenge, I turn to see not just Steve but band and crew to a man. They are all keen to be called from the bench.

The enemy, from a culture of 'I drink, therefore, I am', is stunned in the face of its own kind: my team has obviously had the most to drink and, therefore, is bound to be double hard. The enemy immediately turns on its heels, flees to the car and drives off with an urgent sense of purpose.

Now, no one is jollier at the prospect of a jolly-up than jolly old Bonehead and last night's session afloat had been no exception. Although victory is ours, Bonehead has a final contribution to make. The offensive car, now the best part of half a mile away, is still in his sights and, in his mind, still within striking distance. He starts to throw wide-ranging blows at 'it', the car, something. Not one of us is sure exactly what. He sportingly throws his best shots with his eyes closed. We all see it coming, but can't quite get our heads around how he does it: he trips over the front thirty feet of the tour bus, which Steve has cunningly disguised as . . . a sixty-foot-long, brightly painted . . . tour bus. Careful, Bonehead, don't fall over. But sometimes that's the only course of action open to a man, and Bonehead does, indeed, fall over. He falls headlong into the gutter. It's a selfless act of gallantry and there is not a man among us whose heart does not sing with pride as Bonehead goes the extra mile.

Actually, this attitude is not peculiar to Bonehead. Noel, Liam, Guigsy and Alan would not hesitate to get behind you in a street fight without thought or concern for personal safety. Sometimes, however, the danger comes not from external forces, but from the enemy within.

Twenty minutes into the homecoming tour, the album, *Definitely Maybe,* is number one, the nation is already in disarray . . . Oasis are mad for it.

CHAPTER 11

SLEIGHT OF SOUND

...What hope is there to seize
That mocking image? What thine arms would fold
Is nothing!
METAMORPHOSES, OVID

AS LUCK WOULD HAVE IT, on arriving back in England, the first thing in the itinerary was a night off. Even better, the Bootleg Beatles were in town – unmissable! Where most cover bands bash out their approximations of other people's hit records to two drunks and a Jack Russell in a bar, the Bootleg Beatles have elevated the art of musical plagiarism to a different plane. Firstly, they make a good living out of it. These guys aren't playing for a couple of pints and yesterday's sausage rolls. In Southampton they were performing at the Guildhall to a packed house, exactly the same venue that Oasis, with the fastest-selling debut album of all time, would be filling and thrilling the following night.

It's theatre, with costume changes and period instruments, an exercise in nostalgia. The *faux* four don wigs, glasses, whatever accessories are necessary, to complete the illusion perfectly that up on stage is the most successful pop group in history, and not a quartet of middle-aged men in greasepaint and fake moustaches who don't much care for reality. It had entertainment written all over it. And, as the lovable mock-tops entered, nobody was showing their appreciation more enthusiastically than the famous five mad Mancs: Oasis, a'hootin' and a'hollerin', the greatest rock 'n' roll band in the world, 1994 edition, were twelve rows back ready to embrace their cut-and-paste idols. It was all a little weird.

The audience for the Bootleg Beatles is as you'd expect: 2,000 of those who had loved them when there was still a 'them' to love, beer was tuppence a loaf, it snowed on Christmas Day and John was alive. God bless you, John. I, for one, remember exactly where I was and what I was doing on 8 December 1980:

I step on to the bus, unsurprised that its driver is Dr Winston O'Boogie. The bus is empty and no other passenger steps up with me. We pull away and glide randomly through the deserted streets of Weston-super-Mare, a town that smells of Blackpool and decadence – which isn't to say I don't like it. John Lennon, alias Winston, and I engage in utterly trivial and inconsequential small talk. The bus finally pulls up next to the town's floral clock and, as this journey ends, I turn and, over my shoulder, offer, 'Thanks for the ride; see you later.' Lennon smiles: 'Yes, I'll be back.' I wake easily, the dream gently burned in the waking like a retained image of light when eyes are fresh-closed. Of habit, I turn on the television . . . 'John Lennon was gunned down last night on the sidewalk outside his New

York apartment building.' It hits me immediately: the time slip between East Coast USA and Weston-super-Mare allows for the possibility that death and the picking up of a solitary passenger could have been a moment of synchronicity.

Not many of you reading this will have ever seen the fabs and, of those of you who have, few will have been able to hear what was being played in the days when a good night out with the girls was hardcore screaming and pissing in your pants in row twenty-three. No T-shirts on sale then; all you took home was a memory and the acrid stench of ammonia.

To their great credit, the Bootlegs reproduce the Beatles' songs in the original sense of live, not a Milli Vanilli 'live' experience. The Bootlegs are up there doing it real time – no loops, no tapes, no bullshit. The songs sounded wonderful that night, even through an inadequate PA. Here's a thing, and I steal this lock, stock and barrel from Noel. What if the Beatles had still been doing it live in the latter stages of their collective career, and if someone had recorded just some of it on a half-decent night . . . with half-decent equipment? All right, it smacks of 'if the horse hadn't stopped for a piss, it would have won the race.' Worth a thought, none the less.

* * *

After the performance, the prospect of a closer look is irresistible to Oasis and so we drop into the dressing room. During the show, under the confusion of stage effects, aided by the borrowed familiarity of movement stolen from newsreel, the Bootleg Beatles could have been coming at you straight from Holadeck 1, USS Enterprise; backstage, under the harshness of unforgiving striplight, not so. This magic is not the stuff of Arthurian legend, but rather it is the kind done with mirrors and sleight of sound. Robbed of all this, these guys can only be a disappointment and, sure enough, they disappoint. Although . . . the player masqued as Lennon has not had time to slip out of his costume and is still very much in character. This is all a bit too much for Liam. As he sits drinking tea with the mimic, even knowing that it isn't really his hero (he must realise this, right?), throughout their conversation he addresses the false prophet as 'John'. Liam is struggling to decipher the muddled symbols this evening has thrown at him. It is as if he wants desperately to believe, to buy into the fantasy these charlatans are peddling. As we leave the dressing room, an unconventional farewell (''Ere y'are, John, you cunt, you've done my fucking head in!') is delivered in genuine awe by the unanchored Liam.

* * *

Bonehead, Tony and myself concluded that evening in a curry house where, coincidentally, Virtual George and Virtual Ringo were enjoying a little *murgh tikka masala* themselves. They looked just as unhappy in mid-life as the genuine articles always seem to – spooky, eh?

Cue pretentious disc jockey, c.1973: 'Now it's time for Oasis to

unleash the power and majesty of rock on a sleepy seaside town .
. . great band, Oasis . . . personal friends of mine.'

Wednesday, 30 November 1994. For the first time in their history, Oasis become a full-production rock show with a big, shiny lorry full of new toys. No more dicking around with substandard sound systems and lighting rigs. There was finally money in the kitty, and Marcus and Alex had gone shopping.

The band were edgy and barely able to contain themselves: attitude turned full on.

* * *

Liam, never one to be sitting around reading a book when there's a little hell to be raised, is all caged tiger, prowling the foyer and bar of the Polygon Hotel, emotions coiled tight, fists balled, occasionally shadow-boxing with whichever voices stalk him. Bonehead takes refuge, as is his style, in domesticity. He searches out an iron and board to carefully press and re-press the check Ben Sherman that will share the sweat and limelight with him tonight. Guigsy rolls another joint. Tony keeps himself to himself, locked in his room away from the killing zone, which, increasingly, is whenever and wherever he and the band are together. This is fine: they all know they'll get him later. Noel just sits at the bar sipping gin and tonic, hanging with the Abbot. He is in no doubt whatsoever that his band will deliver. Conversation is not a feature of these moments so I drift into the reception area. White plastic letters are slid into place on a welcome board by a bored receptionist: a conference on infertility is scheduled in the hotel this evening. I smile at the thought of the band returning to the hotel much later on to conduct their own experiments in this field.

* * *

The actual performance that night was secondary to the fact that they were there at all. It was that point in the ascendancy of any destined band where the opportunities to see them play in a venue that doesn't need its own subway system are fast running out. It was obvious that you were never going to catch them down at The Three Ferrets public house again, not even for a beer and a game of dominos. Now you see them, now you don't: the glass wall that celebrity loses itself behind was sliding silently shut. If you wanted to see Oasis other than on TV, across the pages of the world's press or through a set of opera glasses, well, this was the last chance.

I know the show was a good one because they all told me so. I didn't have time to take much of it in. As is inevitably the way with new toys, things were going wrong – a few very acceptable headless-chicken impressions were offered by the tech-heads. On top of this, the paramedic crews of the St John's Ambulance Brigade were getting a lot of unwelcome business. The Oasis audience were appreciably more imaginative than those of the Bootleg Beatles the night before. What that actually meant was that, at 8:30 pm, Oasis and Wunderkind Liam clocked in for another tough day in LaLa Land. At 8:30 pm plus one second, the joint went berserk. Most of the front four rows, an energy brew of youth and whirling thrash-dervishes, broke and collapsed. Rows five to eight filled the gaps, trampling the early casualties with no thought or aim other than nearer my gods to thee. St John was rushed off his feet and there was a certain cyclic beauty in all of this as the walking wounded rushed straight back in where angels fear to tread and, before too long, were being patched up again. The same bruised young faces, eyes glazed in ecstasy, rode this painful roundabout five or six times.

The nuts and bolts and bits and bobs that frame the show were snugly packed inside their mobile home. And for us? Just your ordinary, everyday after-show activities. A few beers in the dressing room; a few more at the hotel; a few more lines; a naked girl intentionally lost in sleeping corridors, hoping that Liam would find her, but settling, if I remember, for her boyfriend. Just as well: better to rock the cradle of love than rob it.

* * *

Southampton to Sheffield. Suddenly, there is method behind the seething madness of Ben Winchester. The band's agent has routed the tour through all towns beginning with the letter 'S' — brilliant! Zig-zagging up and down the country alphabetically not only doesn't stand up to close scrutiny, but can't even be defended at arm's length with both eyes shut. The plan is, obviously, that there is no plan. And it was ever thus – rock 'n' roll, bro.

Our day in Sheffield is remarkable for two things. Firstly, I am given a reminder (if any were needed) of how helpful figures from the past are to the smooth running of a tour. On the road with us from Southampton is a long-time cohort of Liam's, a lovable rogue. We stop at a service station somewhere in our great nation's heartland, a serious misnomer for the killing joke that is Birmingham. The aforementioned rogue indulges himself in a little light shoplifting, which, I believe, is filed under 'Arts and Crafts' in Manchester. He isn't caught, except by me, and I don't count . . . I'm not the filth. He really doesn't get it: how utterly lacking in glamour it is to steal a trinket because it's there and because he can, and the implication by association for Oasis. If anyone gets on the bus, for that period, to all intents and purposes, they become part of the tour. For that reason, I have a responsibility for their actions but, all in all, I might as well have saved my breath.

Second incident of note that day, and one more in keeping with the band's headlong rush towards world domination, is Liam's first look at Sheffield Arena. Noel has buggered off to Johnny Marr's favourite guitar shop to try to avoid accumulating too much wealth. Marcus decides to show Liam where the next phase of the Meisterplan lies. Sheffield Arena is big, cavernous, and Liam cannot believe that Oasis as an attraction are capable of filling it. Marcus and Simon Moran, the band's promoter in the North, assure him that it is a done deal. Liam steps out on to the empty stage, looks straight into the whites of an imaginary fan's eyes . . . not at the front, but at the back of the hall, a hundred light years away . . . he points at the figure, visible only in his mind's eye, screams one word ... 'C'mon!' ... and I believe, somewhere, the acolyte hears him.

Oh yeah, Noel buys three guitars and gets sod-all change out of £9,000.

CHAPTER 12

GROANGREASER

The trouble with the rat race is that even if you win you're still a rat.
LILY TOMLIN

COSMIC FORCES WERE ALIGNING, or something along those lines. The trappings, rewards and nefarious gains that go hand-in-cloven-hoof with success in the Music Biz had begun to manifest themselves: somewhere not far from a dusty crossroads, a tall, pointed man was laughing at a signed contract.

Assembling the guest-list for an Oasis gig had, up until now, been a straightforward process and the list was rarely extended beyond double figures. The favour of a backstage after-show pass tended to be restricted to cousins, uncles, sisters and brothers. In its restriction, the favour was also extended to the band's new best friends who, not uncommonly, were the local drug dealers. (What is it with small-time pushers and acne?)

I have fairly extensive experience of this element of the criminal classes. Drug dealing as an industry is a predator-infested, primordial sludge. We only ever exchanged niceties with the amoebae therein. So who is the typical junkymonger? See the scraggy creature there in the shadows: pretentious haircut; eyes like grubby loose marbles that never look you in the eye; a spotty chin rubbing against a cheap mobile phone? He's as sharp as a hot-water bottle, tries too hard to please, sniffles names and drops them. There's a major deal in the mix, but there's always a major deal in the mix. And he bores like a scab that refuses to pull from the skin.

The employment of Coca as a masticatory goes back to the time of the first Incas, being used in their religious rites as an offering to the sun; the sacrificing priest never consulted the oracles without holding some Coca leaves in his mouth, and throwing some into the fire which consumed the victims. (*Coca, Cocaine and its Salts*, Martingdale, 1886.)

Of course, drugs and popular public figures have lived alongside one another since popularity meant money; and money, in turn, brought access to a more experimental realm outside the engineered taboos of a so-called well-ordered society. The small-time peddlers of the exotic are there because of this strange attraction, and so it would be unfair to lay the blame entirely on such sad and sorry heads.

Of late the importations of *Coca* into London, Liverpool, Havre and Hamburg have overstocked the European market. Some of it comes in tin-lined cases containing two tambores, but most of the large leaves (Bolivian variety) still arrive in rough canvas bales, generally lined with waterproof tarpaulin, and weighing from 120 to 150lb. each, two of which it is said form a load for a mule for transportation through mountain passes or across the Andes for exportation. Cocaine and its salts, although selling at one time as high as 3s. 6d. per grain, are now reduced to a very moderate price. (As before, Martingdale, 1886.)

The first clues that the band's official rating on the international liggometer was seriously on the rise came after the gig in Cambridge. Sheffield had thrown up Mike Joyce, erstwhile drummer for The Smiths and Public Image Ltd, but Cambridge gave Oasis their first experience of rubbing scrawny shoulders with some serious late-night company. Chrissie Hynde was there – on balance, a good thing – and Mark E Smith brought more points to our side. And then there was Patsy Kensit – hello – Ms Kensit and the Burnage boys? Something's in the air.

However, the real proof of the climbing Oasis media appeal was in the pudding baked a couple of days later in the well-ordered halls of the British Broadcasting Corporation. Once the gig in Cambridge was done and dusted, and the Great and the Good had kissed each other's arses, we got the fuck out of Dodge, did the overnight thing and shot our load down the M11 to London, to an altogether more confident peddler, the *vivandière* offering extra: Paula Yates. More of that later.

The next gig on our list was at Glasgow's Barrowlands, one of the greatest venues on the UK touring circuit. It is Glasgow incarnate: a place of the people for the people where natural light hangs up its hat at the door. It sits like an octogenarian wearing too much make-up that couldn't give a shit, a heart cast in 24-carat gold. The night Oasis took themselves to the Barras was a busy little affair, sending messages and signals to presage the recklessness with which the gods of sex, drugs, guitars and a chemical diet satisfy their appetites for tragedy. But before that, there was real work to do. Real work for Oasis is the business of selling themselves. Shooting a video, for example, counts as real work and it was that time again.

Irvine Beach, Scotland, Friday 14 and Saturday 15 July, 1995. Two of the greatest rock 'n' roll shows I've ever seen.

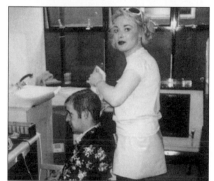

Above: Bonehead receives a make-over prior to appearing on music TV show
The White Room, December 1994. He emerged, bewigged and bewitching, as the
artist formerly known as Bonehead.

Below: With his twin from Sesame Street, backstage in Japan.

Above and opposite: Shots from the video shoot for 'Whatever', 5 December 1994.

Below: Oasis ex-drummer Tony McCaroll.

Slane Castle, near Dublin, 22 July 1995. It should've been a great day – the one that got away.

Life's a beach, and then you do a cover shoot on one. On location for the single sleeve for 'Roll with it', Weston-super-Mare, 21 June 1995.

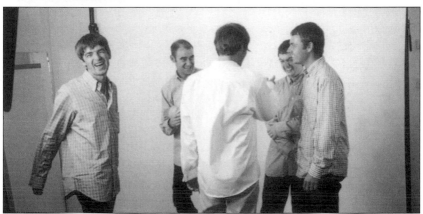

Clockwise from top left: Nearly the cover shot for 'Wonderwall'; Liam and crew member Jacko in a helicopter: shiny happy people: Noel with Paul Weller, (to Noel's left) rehearsing 'Talk Tonight' for The White Room, April 1995.

Clockwise from top: Noel and Bonehead's bluesathon; Noel is elsewhere finishing (*What's the Story*) Morning Glory?; hanging out at Slane; Robbie Williams backstage at TOTP – two phones so we can order twice as much!

Clockwise from top: Liam and Bonehead talking about baths; Noel alone, a loner; Sid Cox trying to sell swag in Japan; Liam and Noel pose for the *Observer* magazine.

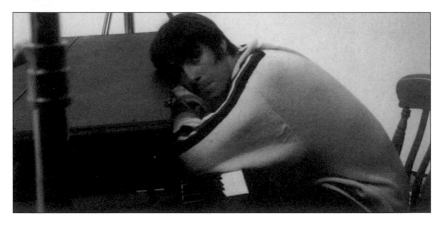

Clockwise from middle left: Liam: chilling; underwater in Roppongi Prince Hotel's pool, Tokyo, 25 August 1995- thing were less tranquil when everyone got their kit off later; drunk in charge of a Union Jack; when he was good, he was very, very good.

From its first naïve outing on MTV, the song 'Whatever' had grown up. An arrangement of strings had added a sophistication that Noel had perhaps never imagined, but was now taken for granted as a natural development. Before we went north, the band had to endure another day of 'cue lights, cue sound and ... cue action', to tart up the new single into something agreeably coquettish for MTV and its fickle counterparts around the globe. The run from Cambridge was high octane. A 'people's' baron, white-trash scuzzy and slime, had come up with the goods.

You might be astonished at how often a band like Oasis – so celebrated in the media as a permanently wasted testament to doomed, druggy youth – sit around nursing warm lagers and cold pizza before having an early night because the drugs didn't show. The reason given is always the same: the dibble has just put a major bust in. In fact, the adolescent dope lord is frequently just plain incompetent.

All drug weasels, I suppose, possess a cunning of sorts, but it's not going to split the atom. One remembered character was dumb enough to smuggle a *pissant* amount of cocaine into Rio de Janeiro! With hindsight, I guess he was as safe as houses. If the Brazilian customs officers had arrested him, they would have been obliged to let him go, given that the rubbish marketed as hooter in London rarely has any detectable drug content in it at all, and it is perfectly legal to import talcum powder and Ajax anywhere in the world. Clearly, arithmetic wasn't his forte: a gram of coke to a small-time dealer in the UK probably costs around £40 before they tread all over it and push it out for £60–70 – a tidy little turn. In Rio, a gramme of king hell (that's enough about me, let's talk about me) – real, bluey-pink, flaky rocket fuel – costs $15. Hmmm, a shrewd businessman is Johnny Smalltime, so I'm told.

* * *

Inside the big white bus charging towards London, long white lines are racked across all available surfaces. We come all flat top, we got separate hi-fi, we got home from homing, we got blasting beetles, they say Ab-bey Road, Let It Be, Double White Revolver, we got MTV, come together, right now . . . over we. A bizarre Mersey mosaic. Together, the band, the crew, management, and the ever-present and growing retinue of celeb-satellites, make up a total of twenty opinions. The twenty opinions are varied, and are being shouted in competition with the surrounding sonic maelstrom. It would be easier to sleep in a washing machine on spin. We arrive at the Copthorne Tara Hotel in Kensington at around four in the morning and, given that, in these strange days, enough is never enough, a room is designated and the new dawn is seen through the skewered paranoia of cocaine eyes.

There is to be a second run at the video for 'Whatever', the first attempt having been aborted when Liam refused to show. He had claimed that his absence was a one-man protest against the puerile nature of the script. But we all knew that he had got himself badly fragged the night before. He had, in fact, approved the very same 'puerile' script weeks earlier. No doubt his casualty status and newfound political activism were not unrelated. Boys will be boys. Liam's single-mindlessness in marching behind a banner of quality control had cost Oasis £20,000 in cancellation fees. Noel was not amused.

Call time is 3:00 pm. Frankly, there is no chance that the band can be expected to appear on set before this – they just won't get out of bed. Bonehead, Guigsy and Tony arrive together in the lobby. They are as punctual as usual, which is to say sort of on time, not very late. Noel is bedded down with Rebecca in Maida Vale and I am going to pass by in a car to pick him up. Liam, despite his assurances to the contrary, has failed to show. Once again, the other band members are left to kick their heels. I go upstairs to do my Mr Unpopular thing with a pass key.

Liam's room is the familiar combination of sights and smells: emptied mini-bar miniatures of Jack Daniel's, Bacardi, vodka, brandy and gin. Campari . . . ah, this has been a really late night. Stuffed ashtrays, now smelling like refuse trucks in a heatwave, rasp in the air along with a hint of clammy clothing that hasn't seen a wash cycle since the last trip home to Main. The curtains have been pulled tight in an unsuccessful attempt to ward off painful shards of sunlight. Last, but not least, is the inevitable dishevelled girl in his bed, hair showered across the pillow.

'Liam?' I think a direct approach is best.

'Eh?'

'Liam, it's Robbo. Time to get up.'

'Aaah, Robbo, fuck off.' Liam rolls away from me and grabs the girl.

'I can't fuck off. You've got a video to do.'

The girl moves and opens her eyes. Liam puts on a pained look. 'Can't do it . . . my voice is knackered . . . badly, badly.'

'Sorry, chap, you can't blow this video off again.'

Liam thinks about it. 'I'm not doing the video, I...'

'No use.'

'What?'

'This time you have to do it.'

A new line of reasoning now comes into play. 'Come on, Robbo, how could you get out of bed with this in it?' He nods at the girl. She blushes and smiles.

I smile. 'Yeah, she's lovely, but she wouldn't be there if you were a greengrocer. So let's go to work.'

Liam laughs and tells me to fuck off again, but I know I've scored and that he will be down.

The set for the shoot is a white infinity room. Other than the band's tools of trade, it is empty. The impression is that of guitars, drums and amps suspended in a pale universe. Oasis lean on Lucozade to help them through the first rough hours of hangover. Their stark surroundings viciously reflect the brutal payback that is chomping like Pacman through their brains. Film lighting doesn't help. Noel is engaged in conversation with the conductor and arranger of the strings section. This is new territory for a songwriter brought up on popular media. His usual confidence deserts him a little as he runs through ideas with a 'real' musician. Indeed, the strangest and most lasting image of the day is of Noel and his developing relationship with these classical artists. He is thrilled by the added dimension brought to his song by the strings, a musical maturity enjoyed by all the members of the band. As the rich timbre of violin and cello stirs around the song that will mark the band's first serious assault on the Christmas charts, Noel hunches down into a comfortable seated position, jammed between two monitors, with his head resting on his hands. Seeing him watch the ensemble run through its parts again and again for camera rehearsals, I bet that this is one of the single most rewarding moments of his life so far.

*   *   *

Shooting a video is, for the most part, endless hanging around. The studio is always slap in the centre of nowhere and, invariably, it rains. Already Oasis had a dirty name and reputation within the small and incestuous world of film production, and it was clear throughout the day that the assembled film crew were nervous. The band, though, were no more or less grumpy or hungover than normal. The hours ached by without notable incident.

CHAPTER 13

CURB CRAWLING

Only when men have got all they want can we tell who among the crowd has taste or not.
CRITIQUE OF JUDGEMENT, IMMANUEL KANT

THE PRESENCE OF MANY fab and groovy hipsters in the Oasis dressing room at Cambridge was also an unfortunate indicator of the approach of a new set of admirers, attracted by the band's increased hip quota.

The media whore. This creature, male or female, is found sniffing around wherever the newest and the shiniest gather. Usually, it is a few years older than those it seeks to be seen with, using them to enhance its own tiring image. By nature, nocturnal, carnivorous. Not quite able to make it into the big league. Tricky to track down, its lair unpredictable and changing. Arcing from Ladbroke Grove des res – lazy weekends spent flicking through tabloids looking for itself – to first-class airport lounge. It prefers artificial light to the sun and has a particular love for the flashing embrace of its cousin from the same family, the paparazzo.

Patsy Kensit certainly isn't a media whore. She's classy, a more elegant kind of gal altogether. Chrissie Hynde had brought her to see Oasis as part of a girls' night out, unbeknown to any of us at a time when her marriage to Jim Kerr of Simple Minds was unsteady. She fizzed around and was clearly vibed up by the show she had just seen. Suffice to say, the brothers Gallagher had 'noticed' her; let's face it, there are less attractive human beings than Patsy. Most of us, in fact.

As the band put the filming of 'Whatever' behind them, and lined up to continue flogging themselves, they were lining up also for an audience with the awesome Paula Yates. Look into a dictionary of common expressions under 'self-promotion'. Actually, it's not there yet but, when it is, it will be accompanied by a picture of perky Paula – the photo, no doubt, supplied by her own PR.

* * *

It's another day in London, with an opportunity to lie in before appearing live on TV as a part of the BBC's popular music show *Later* with Jools Holland. A very late night has taken its toll and now everyone is locked securely in rented rooms with no immediate fear of interruption. They do not emerge until late afternoon. This is of little consequence as we have no commitments until around 6:00 pm.

It is extremely difficult to position correctly the right time for anything on the road. Too early and everyone is still bombed from the previous evening; too late and the buggers are bouncing around like hyperactive eight-year-olds, looking for something expensive to spill their first drinks of the day over. On this occasion, and by pure fluke, my timing is perfect and, as I drift into the bar, the guys are relaxed and the first round is on its way. We only have fifteen minutes to kill before leaving, for the BBC will provide something to occupy minds battered into vacancy by a routine that isn't, really, and an awful lot of 'hurry up' and 'wait'. There is a wonderful quote from Charlie Watts, drummer for the Rolling Stones. When quizzed about a life of superstardom, he observed, 'Well, it's been twenty years spent hanging about . . . and five years' work.'

A promise of free clothing has been made good by a designer friend of the band. Like all of us with a weakness for instant gratification, no sooner have the tantalising packages arrived than they are shredded by the band, their contents immediately replacing what is now considered old: old because here is 'new', which, of course, must be better. 'Old' is now relegated to another loose pile in some dressing room or tour bus. All five members of Oasis are now sporting evidence of their mate's generosity: sharp, monochrome, simple single-breasted suits! If Quentin Tarantino had not made his mark on modern culture, the sight of Noel, Liam, Guigsy, Bonehead and Tony so crisply dressed, so obviously at that moment part of something together, would have begged comparison with the young Beatles. But Tarantino has passed through, and my first reference is *Reservoir Dogs*. In the interminable Oasis v Blur debate, the press always regurgitates the Beatles v the Stones. I once said to Liam, 'Be the Beatles *and* the Stones.' Certainly in the bar they wear the insouciance of the Stones and wrap it in the stark elegance of 1960s Beatles . . . that's a start.

Drinks were polished off and we piled into the back of a minibus that took us to the White City studios of the BBC. The building has a timeless quality to it – timeless in the sense that, the day after the last 'i' was dotted in its construction, it already looked as ill-conceived and out of place as it does today. Plain ugly.

But we're in, keys to the dressing room claimed. We Indian-file brashly into the building's disheartening interior. That this venerable corporation produces work of the calibre that it does is testament to British creativity. It's as if the building's designer had decided, right, let's make it really tough for them. Two days out of the touring cycle and, despite the monotony of yesterday and late nights, the opportunity to stay in bed has recharged batteries – the swagger is back. We burst through a door marked NO ENTRY and pass from light to dark, moving into hushed shadows. The set of *Later* reveals itself, although probably not to the band . . . sunglasses surgically attached. Even Coyley's playing the shades game: the man who needs binoculars to see tall buildings at short distances has entered a dark room in darker glasses – something has got to give, and it's the sound engineer. He removes the style accessories and squints into the gloom. Oasis, though, continue and, without breaking stride, sweep through and out the other side. No one trips or slips over the countless obstacles a working studio throws up. I think that's pretty cool; if any of them lose the power of sight, the Royal Institute for the Blind can save themselves the expense of a guide dog.

Numerous camera rehearsals are endured until, finally, it is time to film the show for real. Booze is hard to come by at the Beeb, which is a good thing as everyone stays straight. The format for this popular programme is simple, yet highly successful. Conceived, produced and directed by Mark Cooper and Janet Fraser-Cook, it was, from its inception, an immediate winner. All the artists and musicians taking part form a circle facing centre. Throughout shooting, they will remain *in situ* playing not only for the studio audience, but for each other. This egalitarian approach can often prove to be a mixed blessing: we were tucked in next to an all-female *a cappella* ensemble from Belgium.

The show's presenter, Jools Holland, is amiable and user-friendly, with a nice line in practised ad-lib. He has introduced to the set a flipchart with his tips for the number-one record across the UK on Christmas Day, with current betting odds. 'Whatever' is one of the favourites. In a style not unlike copied gameshows around the world, this chart is framed by a blonde in an itsy-bitsy, teeny-weeny frock, a shade of red visible across continents. Mr Holland's sultry, pouting assistant is top poppette, Paula Yates.

* * *

Oasis performed two songs – actually it might have been three. Certainly, they played 'Live Forever' and closed the show with

'Walrus'. Throughout their short sets, Paula was barely able to control herself. Normally self-composed, she wiggled, shimmied and shook with the music, never taking her eyes off Liam.

* * *

Job done and done well, we are gathering our wits in the critical light of the ante-room given to us for chilling out. The door is locked from the inside and the band's favourite coke carrier is racking them out in proportions that would not look out of place in the closing scenes of *Scarface*. This is just a pit stop, a charge to carry them through to the party taking place in the Green Room upstairs . . . and along a corridor, and down some stairs, and then left, another corridor, through a lounge area, double doors, more corridor, more stairs . . . 'Are we bloody well there yet?' . . . 'Yes' . . . 'About time.' It is the last show of the series and the room is humming with artists, first ADs, second ADs, producers, production assistants, guitar technicians, chippies, archbishops, sparks, grips, runners, friends and guests, and friends of guests, and friends of friends, and Paula Yates . . . and Liam Gallagher. Liam has had a couple of lager and lines; Paula is straight. Liam is in conversation with Alan McGee, Tim Abbot and Bonehead. Paula links arms to steer Liam away from the safety of his friends. I am just within hearing distance and can hardly believe the suggestion she has for him.

It is a BBC party, the refreshments are warm and quickly run out. Liam has extricated himself from the thin arms of Lady Geldof and is giggling with his mate Sid Cox. I ring for cars and we leave.

I share a limo with Liam, Bonehead and three cases of Moet & Chandon, a present from Sony to commemorate *Definitely Maybe*'s entry into the album charts at number one. Liam doesn't need prompting. Paula's words hum in his ear like a hornet in a jam jar.

''Ere y'are, it was unbelievable, right. Mad, it was mad.' Liam is happily confused.

I know the answer, but I have to ask. 'What did she say, Liam?'

Liam is grinning. 'She said, right, she said why don't you and me get it together . . . then we can go out on the town and cause a sensation.'

Bonehead rocks with laughter. I half-smile, my worry now that Liam will be in any way interested. 'Liam, she just wants to show you to her friends.'

He sneers his response. 'She won't fool The Kid, I'm on it, I'm wise to it. She's way too fucking old anyway.'

Bonehead laughs again. I am reassured, but this is not the end of it.

CHAPTER 14

DEAR DOCTOR

Whatever I see I swallow immediately
Just as it is, unmisted by love or dislike.
I am not cruel, only truthful –
'MIRROR', SYLVIA PLATH

WEDNESDAY, 7 DECEMBER 1994

Band travel London–Glasgow
British Midland flight BD6.
Check-in twelve, depart one, arrive just after two.

Venue:
The Barrowlands, 244 Gallowgate, Glasgow G4
telephone 0141 552 4601, fax 0141 552 4997

London morning nine, soundcheck at four, doors
at half past seven,
support to be announced.
On the stage at one quarter past the evening nine.

The night before the Barrowlands gig, we incorporated into our act the best and worst of late-night indulgences. After leaving the BBC, our destination was a rented jump-joint off Wardour Street in Soho to help Rebecca, Noel's girlfriend, celebrate her birthday. Formerly a video jock on MTV, and a Swedish network star, Rebecca was fashionably pursuing a career as a dance diva. Noel was circumspect when confronted by the chanteuse and asked for his opinion:

'Interesting, definitely interesting.'

Interesting probably meant something different in Mancunian. I logged it with my lengthening list of Oasisisms:

- *geezer:* jolly good chap
- *top:* splendid
- *on top:* not splendid
- *the dibble:* police

Manc, when spoken by a master of the old language, is as incomprehensible as Glaswegian and Swahili.

* * *

Tony McCarroll has decided not to come. He is becoming increasingly sidelined by the rest of the band and is now almost Herculean in his efforts to dodge the spite.

Although this is no 'bring a bottle' gathering, Noel, Liam, Bonehead and Guigsy are characteristically generous: three cases of Moet and six bottles of Jack Daniel's donated by a grateful multinational corporation (fancy that, Oasis, captains of industry). The party is full of style pigs. They can smell a free drink through a closed door. The warm and tropical regions of the Old World has its vast swarms of locusts and we have ours, with far more expensive tastes. Within ten minutes of our depositing the liquor with the hired help, the plague descends and the whole lot goes. I do manage to hold on to a case of bubbly for the band and Noel's babe. This, too, is eventually drained.

Bonehead and Guigsy have already left the building. It is three in the morning and our options are limited. Roosterfish would have been the shout a few years back, but things change. Things also stay the same. Browns on Queen Street in Covent Garden is a quintessential showbiz haunt. Boxers, footballers, Page Three models and 'actresses', they're all there; it is Rebecca's destination of choice. Liam, Noel and I join her – it's her birthday, after all. The Gallagher brothers are still card-sharp suited, perhaps just a tad bleary of eye, but 'Mad for it, Robbo. Fucking mad for it!' Charlie comes too, but then he usually does. No danger of anyone falling asleep at the wheel ... so to speak.

Entry is swift and we are ushered upstairs by an obsequious hostess to a place behind closed curtains. A scarlet, brass-hooked rope keeps the rabble out, or is it a pen we're herded into? Upstairs, important people talk very loudly, and very, very quickly, about important things – themselves, occasionally looking down at their admirer-executioners. Odd, no sign of Paula. We slump into chairs chosen specifically to flaunt the owner's taste – it is all so tasteful. Understated decor in order that no competition will upstage the consequential punter. The walls are in muted pastels, the better to enhance Versace and John Richmond. Our table is a ragged, oversized pill of aquamarine glass; Charlie should be comfortable here. Later, it will seem as if, when travelling from Rebecca's party to our hotel, we had taken a detour via a Studio 54 of 1974 vintage. Nobody is overly interested in our corner. Noel's songs of hope written from the guttural don't resonate with these people: gutters are to be avoided by well-shod feet when stepping from bright-wheeled limousines. Nobody buys Oasis in Browns in 1994. Noel and Liam don't give a flying fuck what people think; things are going to change. Conversation is easy; brother and brother enjoy their differences and warmly embrace the similarities. It is nights like this that I'll carry with me long after I've discarded the remembered fragments of chemical savagery. *(What's the Story) Morning Glory?* has not been written yet, there is no sign of a number-one single, America hasn't plugged in and, quite frankly, my dear, Europe doesn't give a damn. The time has come, the Walrus said, to talk of many things, and we do, and it is 'top'.

*   *   *

By the time we had gathered our luggage at Glasgow Airport, our only option was to go straight to the venue and the soundcheck. I noticed how hoarse Liam's voice sounded, but put it to the back of my mind. Oasis hadn't played a gig for three days and so I assumed that the strained choke of his speaking was just a temporary effect of London's irresistible temptations. Everyone has had better days. The problem is that, while the rest of the group communicate through hardware that never stays out late, Liam's interface is part of his tired and ravaged system. Guitars can be polished and restrung. Drums thrive on being knocked about; new skins are available and easily fitted. For the singer, there's only so much a hot cup of Lemsip and honey can do. Cocaine is a hard friend in the ear, nose and throat department: it takes as much out of you as you put in. Nobody was worried: Liam was young: he could bounce, couldn't he?

Maybe once, yes. Now his appetites were increasing as availability of the narcotic of choice became less and less of a problem. Sadly, Liam's favourite drug tended to be whatever the hell was available, smack excluded. In his position as an emerging Rock God, he seldom received a bill. A good job, as he was more than capable of seeing off three or four grams of Charlie in a day, and maybe a little E and certainly some spliff (after all, variety is the spice of life). To the paying public that's the best part of £300, 'but to you, Mr Gallagher,' most dealers settled for the opportunity to talk shite with him, and boast about it afterwards.

Anyway, at the venue we hooked up with the crew who had been hard at work since 8:00 am. The Barrowlands has a loading bay that can only be described as nasty, nasty, very, very nasty. It gives you the choice between a flight of interminable stairs or a goods lift as reliable as a submarine developed in the Central African Republic. The house crew, though, were up there with the finest in the land. We had a quick cup of PG Tips after a straight-in, straightforward soundcheck and then left quickly from the underground car park. A Range Rover and a BMW raced us to the hotel. Liam was now even more racked. Nothing a few hours' rest couldn't put right. Right? Wrong.

* * *

Four songs into the set – Liam's been fighting to keep up all the way from Columbia – the drum riser is given a good kicking and his microphone is punch-drunk. If looks could kill, he'd be on his own up there and I'd be searching for four bodybags. Liam's losing it and no one escapes his angry fear. 'Digsy's Dinner' just won't come out; more a donkey's dinner. Breaking point hits as he takes a final swipe at the mic, sending it, with the stand, crashing into the security pit, and runs for his life to the dressing room. The band plays on. Noel steps into the void with an untried and atonal vocal. Bonehead is actually smiling at the chief's efforts, Guigsy wisely looks elsewhere and Tony keeps his head down and goes for the line. I follow Liam to see what we've got. For starters, we haven't got a dressing room. Liam is remodelling the space, starting with the chairs and rapidly working his way through whatever isn't bolted down. His theme is chaos; the technique . . . to pick something up, throw it somewhere else, kick it until it breaks and then swear at it. I figure that the fury will pass and so wait out of harm's way. 'Digsy's Dinner' is over and I'm back at the side of the stage.

Noel raises his hand to the 2,000 jabbering Jockanese. 'Hang on a minute, I'll sort something out.'

I watch him leave the stage. Bonehead, Guigsy and Tony suddenly find their shoes more interesting than at any previous point in their lives. I join Noel and we head to meet the wild one.

'The punters don't care what you sound like, they just want to see you up close.' Noel's grasp on the situation is accurate. Liam doesn't see it this way. 'Fuck off!' He wants to give one hundred per cent, can't accept anything less.

Noel gives up and returns to the stage where the 2,000 are still hanging on. No loaves or fishes: Noel cuts in with a solo acoustic spot as the others huddle offstage to share a stolen snout. I'm yo-yoing again. Back to Liam.

He doesn't have to say anything, his face tells its own story. 'I can't sing another note.' The man is overboard and sinking fast, and the strangled voice makes it obvious that the paying guests are going to get no more out of Liam Gallagher tonight.

Two things must happen: Liam has to get back to the hotel and into his bed immediately, with whatever medication can be rustled up, and the rest of the band need to be 'got out' very soon after. As Noel finishes 'Spaceman', I step on stage to let him know what I'm intending to do. What follows is possibly my finest hour in a ten-year career. I lean towards him, speaking loudly and clearly, forgetting that his microphone is as close to me as his ear. 'Right, Liam's voice is knackered. I think we should do a runner . . . we can be out of here before they even know we're gone.' Nearly right! My words are not well-received and now the entire venue knows what we've got. Noel shoots me a look that spells 'well done, good and faithful idiot' and launches into 'Sad Song'. Not satisfied with this performance, I now try another dazzling suggestion, this time made to Bonehead and Guigsy. 'Why don't you go and join Noel on harmonics?' This is treated with the contempt it deserves, but at least the crowd don't hear me this time. Better cut my losses and get Liam back to the hotel and out of Noel's firing line because, as sure as bears shit in the woods, he isn't going to be happy.

Liam is silent as we rocket through the Cimmerian Glaswegian streets in the Range Rover. At the hotel, I guide Liam straight to the bar. The barman waits and I order a large hot toddy. This being Scotland, the barman knows that I'm not making a pass at him.

'What's a hot toddy, Robbo?' Liam is suddenly curious. As ever, focusing on the moment.

'A little Scotch, little sugar, little honey, little lemon juice — that's it. It'll help your throat, and it'll help you sleep.' The barman duly comes up with what's needed and we take it upstairs to Liam's room. Liam is distraught. Tonight is the first time that the band have ever had a problem of this nature.

'What about the fans?'

'The most important thing, Liam, is that you fully recover. We'll cancel the next two shows, get you to a specialist and, hopefully, you'll be ready to go on again at Wolverhampton.'

Liam agrees. His concern is that his voice is all he has. The only emotion he feels now is fear.

* * *

He has said to me often enough that, when in front a microphone, it's the only time he ever really feels happy, that he's found his place in the world. I think I would have been scared too. Confronted with most of the minor and major catastrophes of life, sleep inevitably kicks in as a safety valve. Liam was asleep almost before I'd left his room.

I returned to the Barrowlands to find that Noel had turned

defeat into a decent draw. Oasis minus Liam were all up on stage and blitzing through the remainder of the set. A promise that they will be back to the hall and play again for free has been delivered. And then we were all heading back to the Copthorne, roaring up Gallowgate before the last chord and snare snap had finished reverberating around the room. In the bar, it was clear that Noel had lapped up the chance to fill his brother's boots and sing his own songs to an audience. He was in an expansive and forgiving mood. When I got a gin and tonic into his hand, I broached the far from small matter of further cancellations. It was all very well to make promises to Liam, but I knew that, unless I got consensus, there would be more bitter and vengeful bitching on the cards. Everybody agreed that the healing of Liam's vocal chords was the main consideration. Broken shows could be fixed. Voices couldn't.

* * *

The Harley Street specialist is a tall, silver-haired, urbane man. He wears an impeccable suit cut by a bespoke tailor. His manner is relaxed. This is my first journey with Liam to take medical counsel, and it will not be my last. The waiting room bears no resemblance to a community health centre's reception area, but then the bill won't either. I have sat in less well-appointed luxury hotels. The doctor has an interesting selection of highly polished surgical instruments and he takes a particularly Gaudiesque model and jams it up young Gallagher's nose. I double-check the name and address to make sure we're in the right place.

Yup, this is the feller. I presume he knows what he's doing; with a steel scaffold hanging out of his hooter, Liam looks seriously unconvinced.

'Now then, young man.' The specialist speaks with the smallest hint of Wales in an easy voice that conjures up those hills and valleys. 'What have you been sticking up here then?' Admirably to the point.

Liam has promised to tell the truth in order to allow the physician to make an accurate diagnosis. 'Nothing,' he replies, innocently.

'Liam?' I now feel like his father.

'Well, maybe a little bit of this and that.'

I decide to help the diagnosis along. 'Maybe a big bit of this, and a big bit of that.' The doctor's inquisitive instrument has laid bare Liam's white and crystalline nasal cavities. They are a lot less like a double-barrelled snotgun; more like the Cresta run. Can't be cheap, a nose like this.

The doctor pulls out another peculiar extension. He fiddles about, fiddles about. Two photographs are taken of the unhappy larynx. A prescription is filled out and Liam makes a lot of promises concerning his future good behaviour. We leave, having made a modest contribution to the carpeting of the doctor's country retreat.

We spend a quiet night in a two-bedroom flatlet our travel agent has located, a stone's throw from Wyndham Place. I step out and purchase the necessary ingredients for more hot toddies. We manage to get slightly bombed on these, smoothly slipping in half a dozen or so each in accompaniment to a Chinese take-away.

DEAR DOCTOR

Tomorrow Liam is going home to Mam. The many-headed tour monster will reconvene in Wolverhampton on 14 December. God bless all who sail in her.

CHAPTER 15

GOT LIVE IF YOU WANT IT

I never come to the end, just another beginning . . . never ending
FROM THE FILM *ULYSSES' GAZE*, DIRECTED BY THEO ANGELOPOULOS

LION GALAHAD REACHED FOR THE NAKED MICRO-
PHONE that shivered unprotected in a still space beam of ice-
cold bleached white light scared the lion king thing bared saliva
drip teeth and tested a frail grail of a fur-lined throat torn from
which the same snarled sweet notes strike home back from licking
wounds in lair back next to the one the river nile galahad smiled
askew trains on track again it just rock and rock it just rock and
rock it just rock and roll on track again violet violence and bile
barely held a finger please to dam the dyke england swing like a
pendulum do time to rock and see what england got

well awwwright is everybody ready we are sorry for the delay is everybody ready for the next band smiling tiny mac curdled looks to pole mac biggun looks to stone dread and the bodies on the naked on the low damp ground in the violet hour to the violent sound and the darkness the blinding the eyes that shine and the voices singing the line on line this is the floor show the clapping hands animal flow from the animal glands in the violet hour to the violent sound going round and around and around and around and i feel the bite i feel the beat i see the dancing feet I feel the light I feel the heat I see the new elite I see the final floor show I see the western dream I see the faces glow and I see the bodies steam see them shimmy see them go see their painted faces glow slow slow slow quick quick slow see those pagans go go go go go

Many drugs (in particular, psychogenic substances), if taken in excess, cause various mental disturbances. These substances react with the user's ability to display normal behavioural patterns within society.

Extract taken from 'Floorshow' by Craig Adams, Andrew Eldritch and Gary Marx this is the floor show the last ideal it pop you list got mass appeal the old religion redefined for the facile futile totally blind mundane by day inane at night pagan playing in the flashing light in the violet hour to the violent sound going round and around and around and around and bodies on the naked on the low damp ground in the violet hour to the violent sound and the darkness the blinding the eyes that shine and the voices singing line on line see them shimmy see them go see these painted faces glow slow slow quick quick slow see those pagans go go go go go

Whilst under the influence of psychogenic drugs, the subject feels the effects through hallucinations and changes in normal behavioural patterns. Such effects can lead to disturbing mental conditions. Marhuana usually only produces mood changes but, in extreme cases, can lead to severe and prolonged mental disturbance.

Extract taken from 'Floorshow' by Craig Adams, Andrew Eldritch and Gary Marx now that's a soundcheck and a show cardiff stage it's a beaten zone incoming round trace elliptical phlegm and rheum 76 is gone but never forget 76 is gone 76 is gone never forget dazed and confused eyes speed behind the random dirty jello projectile nine one one singer gone band play on and the audience part and i search and destroy and the lion comes again no aslan no tales of namia this is bedlam and tails of cats of nine jam them in and tamp them down and cover your eyes their poison out there tonight this crowd are strychnine and satin sicking stone dread stock still bigsy hoods his eyes are on tony rhythm sticks not and a crocodile slips out of nile and covers mac curdled and angrily on and angrily off and apres ski is executed with verve and mani and lion scents his first stone rose and drugs from paddling peddlers are slow gentle steady

Psychogenic substances do not appear to have any therapeutic use. For this reason they are restricted by law as Class-A narcotics. They may occasionally be supplied to experimental researchers; nevertheless, they have long been subject to widespread misuse.

and many sweetened air textured and greylined and singing sex grey-lined and singing sex sex sex sex sex raptor cerisse seen and sought and sent home empty and stained tear leave with steve to a safe place where the nile can float into tomorrow on burnaged thrown and lion can roar gently of great deeds with a new soul to keep counsel london calling london to the underworld and we stir sleepy coffee miss breakfast again take to the great white and go for the jugular slicing a nation in emery shards m50 m4 hammersmith steady steve that's our exit enter stage right right string driven things and coyle uncoils coyle uncoils coyle and coyle and the worry and the nicotine last minute shops for last minute shaves guest-list hell crawling up the nose from under stones come new best friends from yesterday but now it's today and we don't do yesterday so no and not sorry stone dread wife in tow

Whilst under the influence of LSD, the subject may experience visual as well as auditory hallucinations, paranoia and a distorted sense of space and time. However, users are able to retain some sense of reality as most are aware of the induced effects. Repetitive abuse may lead to acute psychosis.

into the gloom palais and police palais and police palais and police next door orwellIain all well and good but who is watching the brothers with a parcel of a tune and good keith will be here he in town with richards and he in town he in town but not in tow and hutchence and the demon spawn of preacher man and nile gently weeps new tune too soon mac curdled can't keep up another croc creeps and covers chasms separate band and batterista noel gloomy browed with superfear whatever not what it is and was or should be coyle uncoils and nicotine and worry and nicotine and worry and nicotine and worry doors at eight so don't be late band on stage towers of orange marshall stacked in fearful symmetry tyger tyger time to put the past behind and over the top again always back to this an acid test a sulphurous testing ground

Extract "...gloomy browed with superfear..."
taken from 'Supermen' by D Bowie

One bright May morning in 1953, Aldous Huxley took four-tenths of a gramme of mescalin, sat down and waited to see what would happen. When he opened his eyes, everything, from the flowers in a vase to the creases in his grey flannel trousers, was completely transformed. 'A bunch of flowers shining with their own inner light. Those folds – what a labyrinth of endlessly significant complexity! I was seeing what Adam had seen on the morning of his own creation – the miracle, moment by moment, of naked existence.' (From the cover notes of the 1994 reprint of *The Doors of Perception* by Aldous Huxley, originally published 1954.)

pay attention they will be asking questions impaled by the beat the polaroid girl spins a photo onstage see it land on lion panting chest feel his hand on you tonight pay your money pay your dues pay it pay it lose your shoes Liam does jesus get off the water you will drown rented light circled and angle strobe out the perception it will work chord crash and cymbal soar lion lead nile follow flowaroundsound and cosset suck venom from the strike the wound swells smelling and throbbing and hurting and weeping just enough nightshade to adrenalise decriminalise fantasise not ostracise minimalise decentralise individualise not homogenise not penalise hey kids shake it loose together you gonna hear something that's been known to change the weather like a butterfly dancing in south america have your fractals ready to chart the chaos and then it go stolen away

Mescalin was originally used by various American Indian tribes for religious purposes. It is an alkaloid which derives from the flower of the cactus *Laphophora Williamsii Coulter*, and the knowledge of mescalin psychosis has been recorded for some time.

Rational anxiety is symptomatic of mescalin use. Given orally or intravenously to normal subjects in doses of five to seven milligrams per kilogram, it has been found to cause hallucinations and mental disorientation.

Extract, lines 16–18, taken from 'Bennie and the Jets' by E John and B Taupin and why no more should there be what you want what do you want for seven pounds fifty be careful what you wish for you might get it might get it might get it meet me tonight on a blue bus goodbye you say goodbye I say hello hello hello hell is hospitality and other people so take it away steve just time to make an enemy before chocs hello jake don't hustle for junk in this house we ain't got it and don't want it donna matter who you are you not yet and where it say you gonna gotta be wanna be to never was do not pass fame and fortune do not collect a life to the toppermost the poppermost been there already liked it so much we bought the farmyard ole mac nile had a way with animal impression sixth form humour and we're the only ones laughing but who the one to be the one to save him

Other symptoms include heightened reflexes and tremors. Hallucinations tend to centre upon vivid, multicoloured lights, regular patterns and animals. Human images are infrequent, but do occasionally appear. Spacial awareness and colour definition is often affected; otherwise sensorium is normal and perception retained.

sunflowers as far as the i can see stone dread
behind the cello you have to have a chuckle
sting in the tale sting in the house love your
song noel yours is crap sting confidence it's
a winning thing

The sensorium is
normal and perception
retained.

the sensorium is normal and perception retained the sensorium is normal and perception retained the sensorium is normal and perception retained the sensorium is normal the sensorium is retained the

S

   E

      N

         S

           O

              R

                 I

                    U

                      M

The sensorium is normal and perception retained.

cast 17 cowcr in a locked dressing room unveiling silly silly silly silly silly silly silly silly silly silly silly silly silly silly silly silly silly silly hats and attitude like fake tan it unconvince sunday 18 december great white heat seeking and homing home manchester and viv remember him someone to watch over me to watch over the matriarchal galahad mrs ma mam galahad when lion left home habit change now he back and his queen unsettles nile pour himself a healer cooling liquid but the lion roars confused and strikes brothers toe to toe to nowhere to hide to toe to toe to nowhere to hide from history shared and hot blood irish mam sips smooth white rum righteously proud of her pride purring almost and unaware of how she effort less reach to unnerve he still going round with that old bag who is father christmas just around the corner a week away nothing festive here family gathered wishing well inside hot light and harsh metal

Paranoia can occur in schizophrenic users, and sexual hallucinations are not uncommon. A full dose of mescalin becomes effective within an hour, and may continue for as long as twelve.

but outside it feel like rain;

CHAPTER 16

OF WIND AND WEATHER

...famed for the Giants' defeat, governing all by the lift of his eyebrow.
ODI PROFANUM VULGUS, HORACE

THE RAIN CAME IN from the south-west and lashed heavily against the window-walls of the Brighton Centre. The few airborne seagulls were tossed about the slate sky against their will. Inside the centre it was no less inclement: another Oasis soundcheck and conflict stalked the stage, an uncredited additional band member.

* * *

29 NOVEMBER 1994

Any way you care to cut it, this is going to be a debilitating day. Firstly, the gig, as ever, will demand its pound of flesh. Secondly, there is an official party for the band at the Zap Club. However,

a curfew of 3:00 am. has been imposed, but only on the band –
talk about hope springing eternal. A curfew makes sense because
we have to travel overnight to be in Middlesbrough for a show
tomorrow. Whether travelling overnight makes sense is academic:
we need to save some cash after the Glasgow debacle.

Brighton is home to a dodgy football team, a thriving gay
community, affluent Bohemia and two of the sickest loadies on
the face of the earth: Bobbie Gillespie and The Throb of Primal
Scream. Only kidding. Actually, Bob and The Throb are good
friends of Oasis and further proof that getting out of town at or
around 3:00 am can only be the bastard scheme of a warped mind.
Nothing personal, Marcus. We can add to this the name written in
blood at the head of the guest-list: Paula Yates. I've never been a
big believer in coincidence.

With everything set up for the show, we slip out the back,
Jack, and visit Marks & Spencer. Everybody buys something.
Bonehead and Noel purchase splendid old man's weatherproof
jackets. Noel makes *his* look warm, enveloping and cutting-
edge casual. Bonehead's looks like an old man's weatherproof
jacket. I suppose the world and his dog is destined to shop at
M&S eventually. Noel has already voiced his desire to see the
support band Ride perform, so we make sure that we get back
in good time.

Noel and I are leaning against the back wall of the venue as Ride
come onstage. Ride's lighting engineer, Andy Watson, is a good
friend of mine and I sing his praises. Noel lifts a beetle eyebrow.
'Oi.' He's having none of it. 'Oi' is a signal to silence. Mark Gardner
shakes and takes us with him into the unexpectedly powerful rush

that is the beginning of the band's set. Guitars hover and hum, droning around a fluid backbeat. And, yes, Andy's lights are boss.

Noel turns to me. 'Fuckin' hell.'

'It's a good job you're good.'

Noel smiles, recognising the truth when he hears it.

* * *

The Oasis set was good, very good, and once again St John had his work cut out administering Band Aids and smelling salts to the heaving fans. The weight of mesmerised hope transferred from the heave, trying to touch stage left, stage right and centre, is resulting now in some grown-up casualty counts. Out there, the line between fun and final is thin. Stiffs at one of your gigs is not a good career move – it was getting so I couldn't enjoy the shows anymore. Anyway, we loitered long enough for most of us to engage in a 'fair exchange is no robbery' scene. On the one hand, sixty pounds, and in the other, granulated self-esteem. Then it was on to the Zap.

* * *

I'm not sure how the space-time continuum works, but one minute it is midnight, the next half past two, almost as if the two events have, indeed, charted simultaneously in a picture of the whole night.

All aboard who are going aboard. Tony is already in his bunk on our tour bus, Great White, which is cool for logistics, but not cool for the band. Back in the Zap, Noel is in the 'quiet corner' and he is ready to leave. Guigsy, likewise, will hit his marks on request. Bonehead, of all people, is into a stormer in the corner with pretty Paula. She looks rather innocent tonight and is offering to send a parcel of swaddling clothes to Mrs Bonehead for Bonehead Jnr. I must admit, I warm to the peroxide pet. Through half-closed eyes, Bonehead assures me that he will be on the bus. But where is the Kid? If in doubt, chop 'em out, head for the toilets and listen for a closed cubicle that doesn't sound as if there's a flatulent duck in there. I find one.

'I'm no faker, right.' Yes, that's Liam's voice and he's not alone in there. 'The others, they fake it, but me, I'm no faker. Is that my line?'

They all are. My thoughts stop at the Formica wall I shout over. 'Liam, coach leaves in thirty minutes. We gotta go.'

Liam comes quietly or, should I say, he pretends to.

It's five to three, and everyone except Marcus is now at the bus and we're nearly ready to roll – mission accomplished. Out of the corner of my eye, I spy Liam. He is off the bus and skulking away into the ether. 'Liam!' As soon as he sees that I see him, he forgets the skulking, turns on his heels and runs. I call out to the driver. 'Wait for Marcus; I'll catch you later.' I now find myself in the absurd situation of giving chase to a Dennis the Menace who just happens to be my boss.

Where's he going? He glances back. I'm not sure if he sees me. He can't outpace me. Where's he going? Soon it becomes clear. A hotel appears and Liam's headed straight for it. It's a nice hotel, wanting to be decadent in the way hotels were, I would imagine, in the 1920s. We run up the steps at the same time and I see a familiar face looking down at us from the lobby entrance. As if by magic, Paula Yates is standing there. The game's up and Liam, panting hard, turns to me, but no words come out. I put a friendly hand on his shoulder. 'Liam, I'm sorry, man, but you have to be on that bus now.'

Liam has recovered some breath. 'I'll make my own way to the gig.'

'You know you'll never get up on time. Liam, come on. Come with me.'

It's obvious that Liam thinks I'm being unreasonable and now Paula decides to dip her paddle in. 'Are you man or mouse?' Nice one, Paula. She's addressing Liam, but he has already moved behind me, following me back to Great White.

We move through the darkness and the unceasing coastal rain, each pace into the wet wind adding another layer to a 'bedruggled' Liam. I wait for the onslaught. Sure enough, a corner and a world away from Paula, he lets me have it.

'Who the fuck do you think you are?'

'You tell me.'

'This is Oasis you're working for, not fuckin' Spandau Ballet!'

'I know who I'm working for.'

'You gotta chill out with it, man. You gotta sort it out.'

The guys from Spandau Ballet are about as chilled out as anybody one would hope to meet. However, I'll be wasting my breath if I point this out to Liam. 'My job tonight is to get you on that bus.'

'You can't tell me what to do. You think you're some sort of teacher. Well, I don't need no teacher. I've seen things you'll never see. You can't get into my head. I'm in my own world. I don't need no fucking teacher!'

Something finally snaps and, for the first time, I give Liam as good as he gives. 'Listen, you little shit. I've spent the last month running around in circles after you . . . after you and your "pop star" behaviour. Here's where it stops.' The wind and the rain and I continue, but Liam is silent and somewhat stunned. 'I don't know what's coming over you; I don't even recognise you. You're disappearing up your own arse.' The coach is now up ahead. 'You're going to Middlesbrough, so why don't you just shut up and get on that fucking bus.'

We cover the last hundred metres to our gently humming transport. I'm silent now as Liam demonstrates an extraordinary talent for filthy and painful suggestion.

Marcus is now on the bus and I mention in passing that he might want a word with Liam at some point between now and Middlesbrough. This happens sooner than later and, before we are out of Brighton, Marcus, Noel and Liam form a triumvirate holding serious counsel, Liam sporadically looking over at me. I sit alone and stare out of a weeping window at the blur of dirty ochre street lamps as they melt in hurried passing with rows of colourless houses like cardboard boxes, shrinking in our wake. Paul Weller's 'Wild Wood' finds me and I lose myself in its sweet sonic undergrowth.

I wake when I feel a hand on my shoulder. It's Noel.

'Robbo.'

'Hi, Noel.'

'It's my band. I decide who's in and who's out.' His words are firm. 'And you're in.'

He probably has no idea how much this gesture means to me right now. This tour is only three months old and already my brain is fractured.

*   *   *

More motorway miles and Middlesbrough was upon us. The Baltimore Hotel was our red-bricked base. Exhausted band members remained fast asleep in their bunks, while the bus jemmied into a barely adequate space behind the hotel. After making sure everyone's luggage got to their room, I left room keys and a note concerning the day's activities blu-tacked to the inside of the bus's stained front window, as was the practice. I then retired to my own cramped hideaway inside the Baltimore. In the morning, a call to Liam's room went unanswered, so I had the unenviable task of going up there with a pass key. Just what I needed to start my day.

*   *   *

Liam's room is dark with an inexplicable smell. The lair of Lion. 'Liam?' There is no immediate response, but I sense that there is something awake observing my intrusion into its space. I try again. 'Liam?'

Liam spasms into upright: 'Get out of my room! Don't you ever walk in on me. Piss off, go on, fuck off, get out!'

'I'll see you in the lobby.' What else could I say?

Liam and I circle each other throughout the day, occasionally bumping together like battling tops. When we do communicate, sparks fly as if from jump-leads rudely connected to opposite poles. Even without me, Liam spits at everyone like a skinned-alive bobcat thrown in a salt bath.

As ever, the rest of the band are finally sucked into Liam's emotional whirlpool, four long faces grouped in brooding silence. Almost time to travel to the Town Hall. If half of the pent-up angst collectively displayed in this lobby is released from the stage tonight, the good people of Steel Town are going to get lobotomised and a whole new generation of nightmares will be spawned. Maximum points for creative tension.

The fifth face, *the* face, flames in. 'My room, right?' Liam points an aggressive finger at me. 'My room is my room, right?'

Noel has had enough. 'Give it a rest, will you.' It's a challenge, not a request.

Push does, indeed, come to shove, and shove twists and toys with the idea of ABH. I step into the vortex, take Liam by the arms and force him into the wall. 'Stop it.' I say this without anger, without any inflection in my voice whatsoever. Meanwhile, Noel walks out into the cold northern night and disappears, taking his Les Paul with him. One hour before the show.

Liam hasn't finished. 'If you ever lay your hands on me again, I'll call the police.' Ironic that Liam Gallagher, The Kid, The Wild One, is turning to the dibble.

A mini-bus pulls up outside and we all get in. I drop the four of them off at the venue and then ask the driver to return, to retrace our route, and my eyes are peeled in search of Noel. For once, the India Rubber grinning thing seems to be feeling the weight of events. The M&S jacket looks as incongruous now on him as it did on Bonehead. Noel is storming along a deserted pavement with just the weather and his guitar for company. I slowly step from the mini-bus as it crawls by the kerb, and I'm not sure if he'll run away when he sees me.

'Noel.'

He stops. I can see by the look in his eyes that he has obviously concluded his own post mortem of the previous scene: done his thinking, made his mind up. He raises a weighty eyebrow, gets himself into the waiting mini-bus, and steals himself for the show.

* * *

Ocean Colour Scene were a fine support band. Oasis were OK; there were no guests courted afterwards, apart from two burly pink-eyed drunks whom I ejected. The next day, we went home to welcome in 1995. But there isn't going to be a new year, just last year's dream reawakening.

CHAPTER 17

AMERICA

Poor America ... is it losing the human mind to become human nature. Oh yeah.
THE GEOGRAPHICAL HISTORY OF AMERICA OR
THE RELATION OF HUMAN NATURE TO THE HUMAN MIND, GERTRUDE STEIN

3 MARCH 1995

Dear Messrs. Gallagher

Erm-hi. I don't really know how to start, but regardless of which way I choose to begin this letter, you're bound to think I'm nuts anyway, so here goes.

My name is Lorie K and although we've never met, John (Lennon) has told me that you should have some clue as to who i am and of the role that he says i will play in your future. Okay, before you decide to ring the asylum about some crazy who thinks she talks to dead Beatles, let me tell you about the whole Lennon thing. I'm sixteen (eeurgh) and have been a huge Beatles freak ever since. I have played the game 'existence' to the end and i assure you that I am no novice to the Seltaeb phenomenon. Anyway, three months ago to this day i started talking to John Lennon, first through a Ouija board (groan), then through automatic writing, and now he channels through me and i can talk to him and hear him answer back through me. I also talk to various other people, including Keith Moon, Audrey Hepburn, and most recently, Maureen Starkey. But these are other stories. Now, tho' i'm a fan of your music and love very much your album, the purpose of this letter is not to congratulate you and to gush over your musical talents. Aarrghl 'Happy Jack' just came on the radio and Moony is quite excited. he can be such a vain bastard. The reason why i am writing to you is this – John wants to say a few words to the band that wants to be bigger than the Beatles. Now, whether or not you believe any of this is entirely your decision. If you do choose to believe us, great! And if you think that this is all just a bunch of shite, then fine. I am simply requesting that you write and tell me and John, whatever your decision is. *Yeah. lovie – can i talk to liam and noel now?* Sure, John. *thanks. Liam, Noel, you bleedin' wankers! Your music's quite good, but dammit Noel, stop talking all that shite about becoming bigger than the Beatles! It's nice to be ambitious and all, you're startin' to talk rubbish! I am very flattered that you're constantly singing my praises, but shut up before you piss me off! By the way – 'I am the Walrus' – excellent.*

*thank you my loves! And Noel – no, i would not be writing
'Biker like a fuckin' Icon' if I were still alive. Yeah some of
my songs would probably be rubbish, but don't compare
me to bleedin' Macca! 'Like a Milk Float like a fuckin'
packet of crisps'! SHUT UP! Go back to your <u>Revolution
in the Head</u>. Don't say you wouldn't be pissed if <u>you</u> were
dead and i went around saying* Definitely Maybe *was
the worst shite i had ever heard! However, it is <u>not</u> shite
and i'd be lying if i said it was. So keep up the good work,
you sods! And please no ads in the Melody Maker, Lime
and Joel Gilligan – because i don't want another situation like i had back in 1974 with the 'opened lettuce to
Sodd Runtlesuntle' I'm assuming you know all about my
clash with Turd Runtgreen and i'll say to you what i said
to him: However much you hurt me darling, i'll always
love you.*

    J. L.

    P.S. Liam – i'm sorry you got Select's *twat of the year. that
should have gone to your brother.
– go ahead lovie. i'm finished.*

thanks, John. So, Liam, Noel, whaddya think?

it's not bullshit! Yeah. Alright, then – whatever you choose
to think about this, please write and tell us!

we're <u>dying</u> to know. John

    Lorie K.

anyway, brothers Gallagher, thank you for taking the time to read our little letter and John and i would both appreciate it very much if you kept an open mind about this and honestly and sincerely sent us a reply.

Looking forward to hearing from you soon,

Lorie & John

P.S. Keith Moon wants to say hi.

HI NOEL, LIAM! HOW THE HELL ARE YOU TWO SODS?! NOEL – SYMPATHY FOR OL' PETE, EH? AND LIAM – HOW'RE THOSE <u>DREAMS</u> OF YOURS <u>COMING</u> ALONG, THEN? STICKY FINGERS? HA HA HA!
— KEITH
(the BELL BOY)

* * *

Touring America is different.

Every sense-impression seems magnified until a point of distortion is reached, like living in a hall of mirrors. Even the usual things seem different. The tour buses are bigger and the driver is always a redneck from Tennessee.

The Big Country – America is just *so goddaim* big! Time spent driving between shows can easily stretch to over twenty-four hours. You can go to bed and get up twice, get smashed in the back lounge, and never set foot on terror firma. The America left behind in Utah is not the America you meet in Dallas, Texas. It feels like one nation, not under a groove, but in a whim swing. While you're asleep, an entire population puts on a cowboy hat – drugs are not necessary for this trip. Not necessary, but freely available. Columbian cartels do good work: models of efficiency; a flood of competitively priced product always available. Whether in New York or Nebraska, $150 for an eightball!

America provides you with a new perspective of the industry that's shallow on the inside. In the words of the oft-quoted sage David St. Hubbins, from *Spinal Tap*, 'Too much bloody perspective.' Hurtling around this box of tricks in a road-going liner of brushed *alooominum* is like base-jumping, knowing your chute was packed by an orangutan. Forget space, this is beyond the final frontier.

I love America. I would love it just for the fact that big-headed showers beat the dirt off you even in the meanest of motels and that good filling food, just like Mama used to make, is available anywhere. Everywhere you go, it feels as if you've been there before. And you have: its essential self has been shrink-wrapped and exported by Hollywood to virtually the entire collective imagination of Planet Earth.

* * *

Oasis had just cancelled a tour of Japan and a prestigious show in Australia. Liam had found another 'cause', this time a good one. He felt that the band needed a break and, besides, the arrival of

Bonehead Junior was imminent. Both reasons were genuine: he was concerned for his voice, and he really did feel that Bonehead should be there to see the birth of his baby. Subsequently, an expensive reorganisation by the management brought forward the US tour. Oasis flew to Seattle on 26 January 1995.

* * *

The flight lasts ten hours and forty-five minutes. For nine hours and forty-five minutes, the band drink. Tickets had cost £1,100 per person and, by my calculation, the consumption of free liquor has come close to seeing off this cost. The British Airways crew probably has the worst flight of their lives and I make more embarrassed apologies for 'eccentric' behaviour than Reagan's goons ever did. I speak with forked tongue, each sorry 'sorry' echoed by new levels of stumbling and spillage. If they could stop the plane and let us off, they would.

* * *

Our gig in Seattle was at the DV8, a 'themed' club – the theme; I think, was dirty. Straight away, the tribe at Epic Records were all over the guys putting forward their agenda, which, basically, was meet and greet. These meet and greets – or grip and grins, as we affectionately knew them – were set up by the label as an opportunity for the band to meet the Under-Assistant West Coast Promotion Man and his dog. Anyone who had a role in marketing the 'product' was wheeled out for a handshake and a smile from the *genius loci*. Oasis have never liked it and didn't hide the fact. The label lives for these moments and, at the drop of a logoed baseball cap, can assemble a room full of big, bad hair, loud furred suits, white socks and cheap sunglasses. Almost invariably, these grip and grins are expected to take place immediately after Oasis have come off stage and the band are, as you would imagine, most receptive to bullshit banter and bad breath. The frequency of these events is in direct proportion to the priority level the label has placed on the band. On this tour, Oasis were expected to spin brightly coloured balls and clap for fish every single night there was a show. After the show in Seattle, the band had me designate a corner of the dressing room 'off limits'. Sight screens were erected so that they could hide and, for the label, the whole thing became more a seek and glimpse. Gayle Miller, the tour's promotional co-ordination contact, was not impressed; the meet and greet process as a sales tool is a way of life in America.

* * *

Gayle Miller takes me to one side. 'You know, that could have been better.' Her teeth are clenched, but straight, and very, very white.

'Better?'

'If they want to sell any goddamn records, it had better get better.' A refreshing lack of ambiguity in a duplicitous world.

'Better get better.' She's gone again. 'Better get better, better get better.' I like the rhythm of it. Better get better, better tell Marcus.

* * *

Occasionally, the meet and greet was a huge success, for no reason that Marcus and I ever fully understood. Because of this, Marcus decided to run with it if he could maintain a batting average of one out of three.

After Seattle we went straight to Vancouver and to one of the best Oasis gigs I have ever seen. The venue was at the Commodore Club on Granville Street, the heart of Vancouver's red-light district and appropriately dismal.

The place used to be a ballroom, its sprung parquet floor no stranger to the odd waltz, bosa nova and tango. As sprung floors go, the Commodore's is particularly elastic, a sort of first cousin once-removed from the trampoline. I've been here before with other bands and the stage, which juts out into the auditorium, has a tendency to move up and down with the pulse of the gig. Six inches is the maximum I have witnessed. I mention this to Liam who, being at the centre and out front, will feel this sensation the most.

Liam's riveted. 'Oh, yeah, right.'

The gig is late to start. It is a quarter to eleven and the joint is jumping. It is an old building. Nobody has seen fit to build pukka ballrooms for forty years, and the Commodore dates back to the 1930 – it's double pukka.

I look down at the red-faced, bright-eyed Canadian crush from my position side of stage. A mist of body heat softens the two follow-spots that probe the empty stage in anticipation of the chance to pin Liam Gallagher to the drum riser. Some audiences take a while to warm up, while others signal their intent early on. Here, it seems that every madhead in town is in the building and in a tribal trance. The eighteenth-century English navigator, George Vancouver, might have marvelled at the new colonisation of youth culture, where the new masters are five unlikely lads and the emergent language a creole of fragmented social images and attitude.

As the working-class heroes amble on stage, they are met by a roar like a mile-long mountain diesel thundering into an avalanche. Noel delivers his familiar one-armed lager salute: 'Cheers.' Liam strides in tight circles as he wrings the neck of a tambourine. The only movement from Bonehead is a slight bob of the Adam's apple and a half-smile; blink and you'll miss both. Guigsy gives his nose a wipe as Tony counts the beat in with his sticks. They're off.

They speed double-time through 'Rock 'n' Roll Star' and crash to a halt almost together before instantly powering into the 2/4 sway of 'Columbia'. Big, brutal industrial chords hold the song down around Tony's beat, just as Noel's keening guitar paints a psychedelic line rising like smoke, serpentine, a cobra feeling out victims for the bite. The strain is huge, a circular motif like a slow-moving whirlwind, picking everyone up. Before Liam has sung a note, the lip of the stage is rising at least two feet off true, before falling to rise again in perfect time, as if punched by each note from McGuigan's Fender bass. Liam turns, having been almost catapulted into the pit, steadies himself and laughs out loud. From then on it gets better and better, better and better, better get better.

After the show, we drive overnight, back to the US of A. It's a border crossing, so we're drug-free. Substances aren't needed right now; after a show like this, there is no danger of sleep. We have three fridges on a decent Prevost tour bus, all humming-cold and crammed with slab glass bottles of beer. So we drink and talk rubbish at one another all the way to Portland. Magic!

In Portland, Liam's voice has gone again. Out of nowhere comes nothing, not a sound. Liam responds with all the *gravitas* of a razor slash. For the second time, Oasis fail to deliver as a unit. Abuse is hurled at the stationary tour bus by disillusioned fans as Jason and Phil race to pack down . . . so we can just go. The record label shows an astonishing aptitude for timing and sensitivity by pushing me to arrange another meet and greet. I am not especially polite.

* * *

We did go to San Francisco; we were not wearing flowers in our hair. Liam was taut and tight inside. There have been cheerier 635-mile journeys.

* * *

It is the last day of January 1995 and Jill Furmanovsky shoots stark black-and-whites with Alcatraz and the Golden Gate Bridge as a backdrop. Liam and I race each other along a never-ending pier. The Kid kicks off like Linford Christie, fortunately in baggier trousers. I clump along behind him but, as the pier doesn't have a finishing line, he begins to tire. The gap is closed and the Old Man shades it. We're both knackered and won't be racing back.

The legendary Frisco Fillmore meets the soon-to-be-legendary Oasis and the proverbial good time is had by all. Lars from Metallica is in the house and, after a fine show, is backstage. Noel has his head down signing posters as they are slipped to him.

'Could you make that to Lars, please?'

Noel doesn't look up or miss a beat. 'Like that geezer in the dodgy heavy metal outfit?' Yes, Noel, remarkably like him.

* * *

We travelled overnight again, this time to the City of Angels, Los Angeles, a trip of 381 miles. As it was night, we sped down the Interstate, rather than meandering on the scenic Pacific Coast Highway. Noel and I saw all-comers off to their bunks as we sat up to enjoy some idle pow-wow. The sun was rising somewhere over the nearby desert, somewhere over Joshua Tree. We rolled up Sunset Boulevard to the Mondrian Hotel. Life felt good right then and there, and there was no doubt that we both loved each other and would be friends forever, or at least until the headaches kicked in.

Hollywood, which today is an extensive and thickly populated suburb of Los Angeles, was, only thirty years ago, a bare and desert sand hill, where a few Chinese, Mexican-Indians and cowboys lived among the cactus plants and iron sheds. A great stroke of good fortune came to this lethargic corner of the world, literally speaking, overnight – to be precise, in the night of the 19–20 October 1911. In this fateful night, the first Hollywood producer, Mr Al Christie, transformed with his own hands an old and half-ruined shed into the first Hollywood film studio, by setting up a film camera and a few tattered pieces of theatrical scenery. (*Hollywood As It Really Is*, Dr E Debries, 1932.)

From the outside, the Mondrian looks like a high-rise in an inner-city slum, the difference being that it is a shrine to its namesake, the Dutch abstract painter. The sun is way too bright . . . and way too hot! It's February, for God's sake. Because of this, everyone stays inside.

Even today, we can look in vain around Hollywood for things which the European would consider measures of the degree and value of culture. This town, with its flaunted wealth, its concentration of stupendous fortunes, manages to exist without a theatre worthy of the name. It has very few and very unsuccessful bookshops, and no picture or art galleries. What use would they be? For the thoughts of the majority are ruled by the film, and a literary or artistic film, in the opinion of the Great Moguls of Hollywood, has no chance of box-office success. (As before, Dr E Debries, 1932.)

The Mondrian is close to the Viper Room.

Hollywood is the parvenu among American cities. Its film stars and magnates build themselves grotesque, mediaeval castles, in sham Gothic on its hills, sandy today as ever, surround them with moats, towers, embrasures, drawbridges and walls, and furnish them in fine style with Chippendale and Rococo. (As before, Dr E Debries, 1932.)

No show, but we visit KROQ. In America, rock 'n' roll radio is King, and KROQ is a big-hitter. Much, much more fun is had tooling around the underground car park on a couple of Vespa scooters provided by an LA mod – "course we'll put you on the guest-list".

We're still in LA and kinda bummed out by the heat. The gig was to the max and the hotel is proving to be rad. Marcus has this, like, awesome concept. Some guys have got this bar and they're showing the France v England rugby match. We cruise by to check it out. Inside it's, like, Oxford, dude – real mellow vibe. We're flying, like spacy, man, real – whooah – heavy. Marcus gets some aggression thing going. England win, but I don't remember how. We split after fifteen Bloody Marys. Sunshine can be a drag.

In this pleasantly tempered, not too hot and not too cold air, under the eternally blue Californian sky, with the sun shining cheerily every day and the golden stars glittering every night, well-dressed, clean-shaven gentlemen and beautifully dressed, bejewelled and admirably made-up ladies drive in dazzling motor-cars of the most expensive kind to the studios of the film companies. There our adored darlings, the stars of the screen, condescend with the help of many thousand nameless, half-starving, but film-mad extras, to produce masterpieces of film art for the instruction and amusement of us poor mortals. (As before, Dr E Debries, 1932.)

WHAT'S THE STORY?

* * *

On Saturday, 4 February we played a gig in San Diego. The venue was a nuclear fall-out shelter in a car park. The dressing room was the tour bus. It doesn't get much better than this. We had no hotel, not even a day room. So, to amuse ourselves, we went insane. At the gig, it looked as if it would be reduced admission for anyone with a tattoo. It was good to see Griff, an old mate from the Quireboys, who dropped by with his wife, Heidi. After the show, we drove 375 miles to Mesa, Arizona. This time sleep took us all.

Nile Theatre: day rooms at the Sheraton Hotel, a creche for rock 'n' roll bands. Jason and I wanted to go for a swim, so I was forced to go in search of swimming shorts at the hotel. Americans clearly tend to have generous *derrières*. I bought the smallest size available and gave it my best Stanley Matthews impression. Noel relaxed by busking outside the venue. He made less than a dollar. People need flashing lights and a billboard to tell them something is good. According to my itinerary, the hotel was 1.05 miles from the venue – now there's accurate for you.

* * *

Day off. Hoorah! Salt Lake City! Hoorah! Mormon Central, Monday. Booo! Apparently, there is no need to adjust our watches as we are still on mountain-time. Looks to us like they ought to be put back thirty years.

The gig is at the internationally renowned Bar & Grill, 60E 800 South – just when Oasis thought they were superstars.

We check out of the hotel. Prepared for another thrilling day. Opposite the venue is a supermarket and, boy, folks sure are trusting around here. Little do they know that a gang of professional shoplifters is in town. How do you steal three pairs of Levis from under the nose? Obviously, I wasn't paying attention at school.

Next stop on the tour is Denver, Colorado. Meet two intriguing young ladies: the Velvet Twins. We travel all night, most of the day. Band are fragged and I tuck them away. DO NOT DISTURB signs in evidence on all doors. Night off.

The band play at the Bluebird Theatre in Denver. The previous night, the Bluebird had the pleasure of the Capitol Hillbillies. Tonight they get the good of Oasis Blues Brothers Boys Band, y'all. The support band are, like most of the tour support bands, dreadful. How many REMs does America need? The tiny dressing room has a huge mirror and this is ripped off the wall and put to good use. Just 889 miles to go to Dallas. Oh, God. Three wheels on our wagon and we're still rolling along.

You get on a bus in Denver. You get off the bus in Dallas, approximately one thousand miles later. At what point in the journey do you go to sleep?

*　*　*

The tour bus, a million miles long when we started, was beginning to feel cramped. I had a bunk, but I never seemed to sleep. Tony and I had stayed up the latest. When we were alone, the subject of his position within the group usually came bubbling sulphurously to the surface. There weren't too many friendly faces around him and even fewer opportunities to talk without becoming the object of ridicule once again. Tony had recently taken refuge in the arms of a new girlfriend, an American from Florida. She did not exactly enjoy the respect of the rest of the gang. Given that her first meeting with Tony was consummated with great passion and that she seemed to be totally crazy about him, you could see their point. I thought she was OK. She was now in evidence a lot and this compounded the alienation that Tony was experiencing with Oasis. He began shunning opportunities to hang out with the band between shows, preferring to lock himself away with her so they could shag the be'jaysus out of each other. Ironically, a drum clinic Tony had attended to try to improve his technical act was of the opinion that his problems stemmed from a lack of fitness. I assure you, that wasn't for lack of effort.

Now, as I would carry increasingly rare invitations from the rest of the guys for Tony to join them for a night out, I knew in advance that he would turn them down. Usually, he would answer the door wrapped in a towel, breathless and sweating, another case of coitus very much interruptus. She was certainly a very attractive diversion, but then there were lots of attractive diversions. After sharing the fruit, you have to ask if it's a price worth paying when the serpent expects your soul in return for your place in a great rock 'n' roll band. You have to figure that Tony's time might have been better spent developing his fragile relationship with Noel: more effort on his music and the inevitable politics that plague any tour, then who knows? One of Noel's finer characteristics is loyalty; I'm confident that Tony's position within the group was redeemable right up to the wire. As Tony found his pleasures outside music, screwing away his every spare minute, the only one really getting shafted was him.

Not a day went by now without him coming under attack. Even Bonehead, his old ally, had taken to baiting him. Noel was continually telling Tony that it wouldn't be long before he was back on the Nat King Cole. This was once just a jest, but now it was beginning to sound stripped of all humour and, therefore, more of a promise. In the 'late lounge', an area at the back of the burnished silver roadhog, conversation, after a surfeit of coke (Charlie chat), always turned to the 'Tony problem'. Mark Coyle, who was seen by all as an extension of Oasis, was most vociferous in denouncing McCarroll's abilities. Coyle maintained that the drummer was impacting on the band's live performance. The consensus was always the same: he's got to go. As we thundered towards Dallas, Tony knew that his job was in jeopardy, but felt confident that, at the end of the day, he was still an essential and irreplaceable element of Oasis. But Noel was drafting new songs with more complex rhythmic structures and had doubts as to whether Tony could come up with the required goods.

* * *

We have the Dallas show tonight, but first I am taking Liam to a medical centre. Liam is fearless about jumping off things: stages, balconies, cliff-faces, mountains, satellites. Nothing is too high for him. One acrobatic moment has left him with an ankle injury. We have X-rays taken at the centre and the results tell us that Liam has a bone-sliver floating around in his foot. The doctor decides that Liam needs a walking stick. I prepare to buy one from the tour float.

Liam has the last word. 'Robbo, get me a cool one.'

A cool walking stick?

Noel's guitar is lacerating the steaming air that hangs heavy within the Liberty Lunch. Layer upon layer of calculated scabrous feedback scratches from twin Marshall stacks. It coarses, rubs, like the rusted steel wheels of a freight locomotive. It turns in on itself, and in on itself again, and again, and again.

Liam is rigid in the centre, his eyes laser-piercing a point at the hall's rear. He hammers the life out of a tambourine. Bonehead, Guigsy and Tony drive 'Walrus' along to its regularly beaten and exhausted conclusion. Then, without warning, a midget walks into the inferno – a rocking midget. With his eyes closed and body swaying, he is totally held by the band's crushing rhythms. He has outsmarted the security and is now standing centre stage. He begins to dance around Liam, whose head is now in bits, and asks the singer for the tambourine. Liam hands it over and the midget continues where Liam has left off, beating the living daylights out of it. Oasis struggle to keep up, helpless laughter the only way forward. The crowd are lapping it up. Liam concedes and bounces happily offstage, letting his guest keep the instrument. Nice one, Liam. Afterwards in the dressing room, Bonehead suggests that the little groove machine be made part of the act. With the game over, a terse Noel points out that Oasis are not an 'act'. The circus has acts.

* * *

Next on the list was Houston. We went out to a Chinese restaurant before the show. Noel broke a fortune cookie and it read: you will be successful in all you do. I pinched it – who knows?

We had a day off on Valentine's Day. No cards for me. And then a 592-mile drive to Memphis, Tennessee.

* * *

New Daisy Theatre, 330 Beale Street. One hundred yards away is BB King's blues bar. Memphis ... Elvis . . . Sun Studios . . . Gracelands . . . the Big Muddy. Oasis bring it on home. Presley is a Gallagher icon and tonight they will be touching the legend in the King's own backyard. The record company is particularly well-represented today. Jeremy Pearce has flown in to see the show and there are another dozen or so hot shots from Epic.

Liam's voice is in trouble again. The soundcheck is reduced to rubble. It's Catch 22 for Liam: here he is at the heart of the greatest British rock 'n' roll happening for nearly thirty years, determined or destined to be the archetypal lost cause, playing all the games played by those who went before. The problem is that none of it brings him joy; the only meaningful thing for Liam is the ninety or so minutes in front of the mic. I have watched him burning the candle with different people, in different places, in different countries, time and time again. His body's on fire, but his eyes never catch alight, not the way they do as he lopes through darkness, to lights, to perform. But he wants it all, and all the time, without realising that the partying is killing his music, his art, his gift. It's not fair, is it? Everyone else can rage. Again, their instruments are asleep in flight cases. What Liam should be doing is getting a few early nights. Hey, Junior, behave yourself. But, come on, he's twenty-two, and all the things he thinks he wants are now laid out; the more he takes of them, the more they take of him. He'll never back down as long as there's a party to be had because Liam Gallagher's your man. Thus, Memphis and powder nights have torn the vital larynx and the furniture takes the blame and a beating. The tortured Kid takes time out on the bus and the rest of the band take time to get out, to anywhere Liam isn't. The show does go ahead, but it isn't great. It isn't sold out and this adds a dead weight that makes a four-week tour feel like forty. There are three days to push before British Airways takes us back to change our socks and maybe win an award or two. Until then there's a 710-mile bus journey to Carrboro. Where?

Carrboro. Here. Big student town. Heavy college thing. We spend yet more time in a car park. I go out for pizza. The band are big carnivores: spicy beef is their favourite, followed by Hawaiian ham.

Atlanta, Georgia. Everybody in the band is in a filthy mood despite a fabulous hotel. Bonehead excels himself on our arrival at around 5:00 am. The Occidental Grand on Fourteenth Street is, indeed, grand: Italian marble flights with acres of gold leaf and a central staircase straight out of *Gone With the Wind.* Last night's journey was 380 miles. There were no showers at the venue. The only water on the roadhog is in the toilet. We were looking real good. Bonehead has led from the front on this trip and has drunk the red wine dry. He moved on to beer and, when he finished that, he hit the Jack and Coke until that was gone – our very own Bermuda Triangle. We could have been anywhere and the Bone would have been none the wiser; hats off to Mr Head. Guigsy slings the old soak over his shoulder and the two of them bring up the rear; at this point, Bone is bringing up everything. Guigsy helps Bonehead into the hotel, supporting his sagging weight on his shoulder. The two stagger into a lobby wearing its very best chandeliers, and populated by bellboys who wouldn't entertain lifting any brand of luggage below Louis Vuitton. Once inside, the enchanting Mr Paul Arthurs releases a shattering scream: 'Caaaaam Aaaaaan', punching the air before oblivion claims him. Guigsy is resolute as he steps forward, and manages a nonchalant shrug to the horrified concierge. *C'est la vie, C'est la guerre.* And so it is, to bed.

*   *   *

My own behaviour in Atlanta was less than commendable. I found myself blind drunk – how *does* that happen? – and threw Mark Coyle's birthday cake all over the hotel. It was a chocolate cake and very tasty and I enjoyed what I licked off my fingers. I had my reasons, and they were good ones, but I was responding badly. Noel was absolutely furious and I came very close to losing my job. Time to go home.

CHAPTER 18

DIALOGUES

SCENE 2

DRAMATIS PERSONAE

NOEL GALLAGHER: Charismatic and mercurial songwriter
of Oasis.

IAIN ROBERTSON: Tour manager and security co-ordinator.

WHAT'S THE STORY?

THE STAGE IS IN DARKNESS. A steady thrum of an industrial vehicle is heard. The lights fade up slowly, revealing the luxurious back lounge of a long-distance touring bus. Sofas sweep down either side, meeting at an elaborate console. The console features a TV screen, stereo hi-fidelity equipment, computer games and a VCR. White noise plays across the television and an unfinished plaintive melody is stretching from the tape deck. Damp traces of cocaine litter the Formica surface of a centre table. Empty beer tubes lie discarded carelessly on the floor. A shapeless mound of clothing dominates one corner. Two figures, NOEL GALLAGHER *and* IAIN ROBERTSON, *occupy one of the sofas and are in deep conversation.*

IAIN: These songs are superb.

NOEL: Yeah, I know, but it's like they don't understand. They go to bed when they want and I just sit and play chord after chord until it's right.

IAIN: You wouldn't have it any other way . . . your control, your ego, is based on being the songwriter.

NOEL: (*Affronted.*) Robbo, I haven't got an ego. Come on, I'm totally approachable.

IAIN: Whoah . . . Noel, hold on, chap, how can you stand on that stage, give them your songs with that swagger and not have an ego?

NOEL: Yeah, but ego? Our Kid's got fuckin' ego. What's his problem?

IAIN: Noel, all he wants is one person's approval . . . yours. And I'll tell you, if you can find it in yourself to give it to him, everybody's life will be so much easier.

DIALOGUES

[NOEL is *visibly unmoved by* IAIN's *theory*]

IAIN: Just one gesture from you: to say, 'Liam, nobody could do what you do with my songs.' I don't mean in print, Noel, but to his face, to his heart. I'm pretty sure that'll sort out a lot of problems your brother's having.

NOEL: It's not gonna happen . . . never. I give him my songs to sing. How much more approval does he need beyond that? He gets to sing my songs; that's all I'll give him.

IAIN: That's all?

NOEL *is silent, turns away. The stage lights cut to darkness and the steady thrum of an industrial vehicle is heard.*

CHAPTER 19

AMERICA TOO

And, as his strength
Failed him at length,
He met a pilgrim shadow –
'Shadow', said he,
'Where can it be –
This land of Eldorado?'
'ELDORADO', EDGAR ALLAN POE

New YorkkroY weN
New JerseyyesreJ weN
Washington DCCD notgnihsaW
Virginia Beach VAAV hcaeB ainigriV
Philadelphia PAAP aihpledalihP
New YorkkroY weN
Providence RIIR ecnedivorP
Boston MAAM notsoB
MontreallaertnoM
TorontootnoroT
Cleveland OHHO dnalevelC
Detroit MIIM tiorteD

WHAT'S THE STORY?

IndianapolissilopanaidnI
Chicago ILLI ogacihC
Grand RapidssdipaR dnarG
St LouissiuoL tS
MinneapolissilopaenniM
Milwaukee WIIW eekuawliM

Awwww, New York City, you talk a lot – let's 'ave a look atcha!

Liam and Guigsy are losing interest in Buddy Guy. I'm a fan and *I'm* losing interest; not entirely surprising as this is the point in the show where all the people on the right get to say 'yeah', all the people on the left say 'whoah', and all the people in the middle say 'whoah, yeah'. To stay would be above and beyond the call of duty.

Leaving the VIP box, we slip-slide down to the bar. I order some plastic cups of beer and soon we're all feeling a little more 'yeah' . . . yeah, we're even feeling a little more 'yeah, whoah'. Suddenly we notice that no more than four feet away is one of New York's finest: the original surly youth, John McEnroe . . . you cannot be serious! Liam thinks he has found a kindred spirit and forces his companionship on the man. They hit it off and, within a New York minute, are discussing music. For once, Liam listens as someone else talks.

'You gotta hear my new song, man. Killer!'

'Mad fer it.' Liam is ecstatic, smiling as if this will be his last chance to smile ever again.

'It goes like this.' Mac squares himself to the task of doing justice to his new composition. 'Was it in or was it out?' A tuneless rant leaves Liam gobsmacked. As Mac windmills an air guitar, Liam's chin almost drops to his knees. Mac continues. 'You-can-not-be-ser-ri-ous.'

Liam bursts into laughter, delighted with his newfound chum. 'You're top, you are.' He necks his beer and orders another, shaking his head in bemused joy at the madness of it all.

The following night, Wednesday, 8 March, Oasis play the same venue and in the audience is John McEnroe. Liam had promised him the greatest rock 'n' roll show ever. Mac loves his rock, had sorta heard of Oasis and, what the hell, he only lives around the corner. As it turned out, New York City gets the better of the band. There are two places in the world that seem to intimidate artists, certainly those I have worked with: New York is one, London the other. God knows why.

It is the afternoon in the bar of our hotel half an hour prior to heading across to the venue. I offer to buy Liam a drink. 'Nah, I'll have an orange juice . . . got a show to do.'

A laudable response, but totally out of character. He will almost never go onstage wrecked but, equally, will always have a beer or three. We walk, band and crew together, through icy March rain, two blocks to the Academy and slip through the artistes' entrance. The dressing room is subdued, Liam hovering alone at stage side – silent. NY voodoo? Whatever the hell it is, Oasis cannot shake it and, after curtailing 'Walrus', they troop off heads down to hide. How to lift their spirits?

Fifteen minutes later, the five musicians are sipping beer, listening in disbelief as Epic Records gush over the greatest one and one half hours in Noo Yoik's history. And then our evening is saved. John Mac has crept back; he slips into the after-show mix of gloom and bullshit and says one word: 'Awesome!' Oasis don't believe it, but at least *he* means it – that's enough. Warm beer is discarded, the Jack Daniel's is opened, Mister Happy is back in the hood and, let's face it, there's always next time.

* * *

In the dressing room after the show, the following faxed note was found, sent from Adam Clayton, the bass player with U2:

To Paul McG, Tony McC, Paul A, Liam & Noel

Confucious Say: Never play Philly before NYC.

Agent Say: good for routing.

Manager Say: good for budget.

Band Say May be: but no interviews.

No Sleep till Slane

Thankx for tix and attitude

luv you

CHAPTER 20

DIALOGUES

SCENE 3

DRAMATIS PERSONAE

LIAM GALLAGHER: Younger brother of Noel. A singer of
Noel's songs. Frontman of Oasis.

BONEHEAD: Rhythm guitar player for Oasis.

PAUL MCGUIGAN: Bass player for Oasis.

ALAN WHITE: Drummer for Oasis.

WHAT'S THE STORY?

[LIAM and BONEHEAD *take a bath*]

THE SIDE OF AN ENORMOUS EUROPEAN TOURING COACH. It fills the entire rear of the stage, giving the impression of a white wall of steel with wheels. In the centre of the coach is an open door through which can be seen the suggestion of a plush interior. The windows of the coach are an opaque gun-metal grey, which act as mirrors on the scene out front. The stage is lit in bright light: a midday sunlight. A lazy-legged young man, LIAM GALLAGHER, *is juggling a 1970s World Cup football with his feet, occasionally kicking it noisily off the metal side of the coach. His movements are practised but unsteady, as if he has been drinking. He is wrapped in a flapping Union Jack flag. Suddenly, he kicks the football hard against one of the windows. An exceptionally ordinary voice shouts from inside the coach.*

BONEHEAD: Oi, you fuckin' madhead, give up. I'm trying to read.

LIAM: (*Crashing the ball even harder against the same window.*) Piss off!

BONEHEAD *appears at the open door, blinks and shields his eyes from the sunlight. He is grubby and unshaven.*

BONEHEAD: 'Ere y'are, dick, how long 'til we're on?

LIAM: (*Continuing with his game.*) I dunno; fuckin' hours.

BONEHEAD: I think I'll get Robbo to sort a car out.

LIAM: What for?

BONEHEAD: To get a bath.

LIAM *traps the football with his foot and gives* BONEHEAD *a side-on glance.*

Liam: (*Screwing up his face.*) What?

Bonehead: I wanna get back to the hotel for a bath.

Liam: (*Rolling the football around.*) Whaddya mean . . . a bath?

Bonehead: A bath!

Liam: A bath?!

Bonehead: I mean, madhead, a bath . . . a deep porcelain bowl into which I'll pour hot water...

Liam: (*Exasperated.*) ''Ere y'are . . . 'ere y'are . . . 'ere y'are. I know what a bath is. Whaddya mean, you're havin' a bath?

Bonehead: A bath!

Liam: I know, I know. But, a bath?

Bonehead: I need a bath . . . I want a bath . . . so I shall have a bath.

[Liam *puts all his energy into kicking the football at* Bonehead. Bonehead *ducks and the football narrowly misses*]

Liam: You can't have a bath, slaphead. What's the fuckin' point of having a bath?

Bonehead: (*Now far from amused.*) To lather my body and freshen up . . . sort me fuckin' kipper out. What's it got to do with you, anyway?

Liam: (*Almost turning purple.*) Nobody has a bath! Baths are for poofs. What's the point of a bath? You're gonna sweat all up again on stage . . . don't have a bath.

Bonehead: (*Clearly fed up with this.*) I'm having a bath.

Liam: You're not having a bath.

Bonehead: I'm having a bath.

Liam: No, you're not.

BONEHEAD: What's it to you if I have a bath?

LIAM: You can't fuckin' be in Oasis if you have a bath.

[*Two confused young men,* GUIGSY *and* ALAN WHITE, *poke their heads around the open door*]

GUIGSY: 'Ere, what's up?

LIAM: Bonehead's havin' a bath.

BONEHEAD: I am.

LIAM: Oasis, right, don't have baths.

[GUIGSY *and* ALAN *disappear into the coach again*]

BONEHEAD: I'm gonna get a bath.

LIAM: Whaddya want a bath for?

[*The sound fades as this scene continues without any suggestion of a resolution.*]

CHAPTER 21

MR SATURDAY NIGHT

Oh, what fun it'll be, when they see me through
the glass in here, and can't get at me!
THROUGH THE LOOKING-GLASS AND WHAT ALICE FOUND THERE, LEWIS CARROLL

NOEL GALLAGHER WAS A-LISTED.

Hanging out with Bono and Johnny Depp, it's A-Listing. The listings change, and change frequently. When your mates include Bono, Depp and, let's pick another one, Naomi Campbell, and another, Kate Moss, that's A-Listing. The listings are a media device to quantify celebrities' worth, to weigh and to measure them like the groceries you and I have to shop for personally. There's a B-List and a C-List. B-Types would include the likes of Angus Deayton and Bill Wyman. While on a C-List you might have Terry Christlain, Chas & Dave, perhaps even your milkman. Noel Gallagher, though, was A-Listed. Public people not on any list aspire to C. C-Types aspire to be B-Types, and B-Types dream of the A-List. The thing about A-Listing is that you have to not care, or at least have 'not caring' in your repertoire. Giving a damn, in public or in private, on or off the record, will consign you automatically to looking in at A from the outside. Noel Gallagher didn't give a shit. Noel Gallagher was A-List.

Each time the tour reconvened, after the few days we would have off between legs, Noel had fresh stories to tell of his newfound peer group. He's on the racket with top models.

'She's all right, my kind of bird. She was chopping them out, right, in the bogs, and they were so fucking big they had their own shadows! I swear, right, the lines she racked out cast fuckin' shadows.'

Noel had settled in among rock's elite. Bono and Chrissie Hynde would pop back to conclude existential debates over a few tinnies in Noel's kitchen. Paul Weller, the man most likely to turn into Neil Young and Britain's most authentic blues voice in generations, had become Noel's confidant.

In fact, it was during a Noel Gallagher/Paul Weller collaboration filmed for music TV show *The White Room* in April 1995 that the whole sorry A-Listing just reared its ugly, two-faced head.

The band were bunkered down in the chipboard-and-Formica luxury of the studio's 'dressing rooms' when we once again collided with Paula. This time, the popular authority on childcare had her new, new man, Michael Hutchence, in tow. And that was about the size of it. Michael was in a very tired and emotional condition and, as they entered the building, he was being pulled – with eyes tight shut and angelic smile, barely upright – impatiently by pretty Paula, and then pushed to who knows where. Michael certainly didn't. If *Smash Hits* had presented him with one of their mindless questionnaires, his answer to: 'Favourite colour?' would have been 'Oblivion'.

Noel and Paul stole the show with their rendering of Noel's song 'Talk Tonight'. I don't know: this A-List thing confuses.

Is Paula A-List?

Is Michael?

What Noel and Weller were doing sure as hell was...

For a man whose musical career started on a building-site populated by most of his family, to Noel this was Narnia, *The Faraway Tree* and that place where the elves live in *The Lord of the Rings,* all rolled into one.

I don't think Noel ever went through a day without, subtly and seamlessly, luring any discussion towards the important subject of the Beatles. For example:

'Morning, Noel. Have you had breakfast yet?'

'The Beatles, right, were the best, right, the best fucking band in the world.'

It was uncanny the way Noel could edge a conversation gently in the direction of Fabdom.

''E'e'are, Robbo, listen to this.'

⁕   ⁕   ⁕

Noel is sitting down with his feet up after a tough day being Noel. The phone rings. Can he be bothered to pick it up? Why not: it might be Paul McCartney.

'Hi, Noel. Stella here.' Paul McCartney's daughter. 'We're having a party at home . . . why don't you come over? Dad's here.' Noel is determinedly blasé. 'Well, yeah . . . maybe.' Noel puts the phone down and is ready in thirteen seconds.

* * *

Noel Gallagher stands outside a house, looking at it before going to the door. 'McCartney's house! Paul McCartney's house!' Noel rings the front door bell.

'Hi, Noel,' says Paul, 'come in.'

Noel steps into the house in St John's Wood. Paul McCartney's house. Noel Gallagher is now standing in Paul McCartney's house, next to Paul McCartney. The Beatles, right, were the best, right, the best fucking band in the world.

Paul shows Noel around his home. Thirty years separate them musically, and nearly as many in life, but here they are, side by side. Paul shows Noel pictures, records, Beatles memorabilia, that are to him as holiday snapshots are to you and me. To Noel, though, they are the beginnings of a dynastic history, more precious to the tributary than to the source. If it weren't for this piano or that guitar, there would probably have been no *Morning Glory*. Now they are close enough to touch, to run jealous fingers over. The past is running through yesterday with the future and signals tacit approval.

'I really like "Live Forever" and "Slide Away", Noel,' says Paul. 'Great songs.' Paul pauses. 'Would you like some of this?' It's a joint.

Noel has not touched the weed for years. He has a problem

with asthma, and grass, for some reason, causes havoc with his breathing.

'Thanks.' Noel takes the joint, and a long happy pull on it.

*   *   *

A lot of the lyrics to a lot of the songs on *(What's the Story) Morning Glory?* were written during this period, the beginning of spring 1995. It was a period when the twin vamps of fame and fortune were through flirting with the songwriter and now had hands in his pants and a tongue down his throat. Personally, I expected the messages on the album to be more overtly hippy-happy, but the songs that most reveal the evolution from *Definitely Maybe* show that, to gain admission to the A-List, for Noel, something somewhere had to be lost. Noel's personal stance on his songs is that they are not autobiographical, but then he admits that 'Wonderwall' is about his girlfriend, Meg. Noel also claims that 'no one is Sally'. Perhaps he's right. Someone once said that we cry because of what's on the inside, not because of what we see on the outside. Sally might well be Noel's creation. However, no one writes from within a vacuum, and Sally will be someone or something from life – from Noel's life. One beauty of the song is that we'll never really know for sure. But I'm sure of one thing – someone always has to be Sally.

CHAPTER 22

THE MAKING OF
WHAT'S THE STORY?

No quote.
ANONYMOUS

ACTUALLY, I WASN'T THERE. Anything from me would be hearsay. Apart from...

Noel had been increasingly reclusive in the weeks running up to the end of 1994. On 21 November, in the tour bus outside our hotel in Hamburg, he decided to play the main body of his new songs. It was an exclusive solo acoustic gig. In the audience were Liam Gallagher, Paul Arthurs, Paul McGuigan, Tony McCarroll, Mark Coyle, Phil Smith, Jason Rhodes and Iain Robertson. Noel used a six-string Epiphone guitar, drank Jack Daniel's and Coke, and smoked Bensons. There were no drugs.

Noel Gallagher. Born 29 May, 1967. GEMINI

The tunes were whole, but lyrics unfinished, and often he would just hum or ad-lib to fill gaps. Noel sat on one side of the bus; the rest of us, the other. Nobody spoke one word during any song's performance. Bonehead cried during 'Champagne Supernova'. Noel was not released from the bus until we had heard each song at least three times. As we filed into the hotel at around 3:00 am, nobody was drunk, nobody drove a TV through a swimming pool window, nobody's perception of reality was chemically adrift, and nobody raised their voice above conversation. I would have said it was the most quintessential rock 'n' roll evening of the whole tour, but it transcended rock 'n' roll.

I did visit Rockfield studios while work was in progress – to play football. Nigel Kennedy was in the studio complex at the same time as Oasis and, keen footballer that he is, threw down a sporting challenge: The Nigel Kennedy XI v Oasis XI. I received a call, hit the road and came to underpin the defence; left-back, to be precise.

Five minutes to kick-off and we were missing our inside-centre and centre-forward. Mani, from The Stone Roses, and Liam were seeing off a couple of quick pints by way of match preparation. Nige's team made a studied entrance in matching kit, in matching pink kit, in matching shocking pink kit. Team Oasis were dressed by Savile Rogues. The match began. Guigsy was as good as he always promised; I caused carnage, rugby being my game of choice. Liam scored six goals, one of which curled into the top right corner of the net from thirty-five yards – Roy of the Rovers. The score: Kennedy's XI, 4; Team Oasis, 12.

One other thing: the drumming duties were performed by Alan White. Noel had made good his threat to Tony.

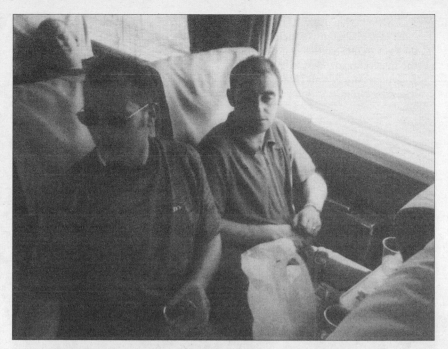

Above: On the bullet train from Tokyo to Osaka, August 1995: Bonehead has a little drinkie with monitor engineer Jacko…

Below: …and wishes he hadn't bothered.

Noel (*left and centre*) watches as the strings do their things for the single 'Whatever', the musical bridge between albums *Definitely Maybe* and *(What's The Story) Morning Glory?*

Above: Soundcheck for music TV show Later- engineer Mark Coyle in familiar headscratching 'somethings not right' pose, the BBC, 6 December 1994.

Below: Onstage at Sheffield Arena, 22 April 1995.

Opposite: Bonehead, suited and booted- Paul McGuigan looks on. Backstage at the BBC for Later.

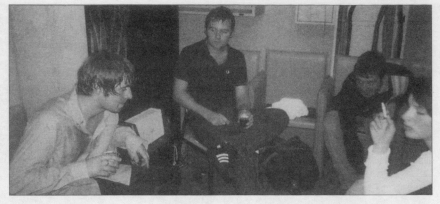

Previous page from left: Tony, Bonehead, Guigs and Liam – a cross between the Beatles and the Stokes – at the Copthorne Tara Hotel, 6th December, 1994.

Top and middle: On the road.

Below left: Guigsy and Bonehead soundcheck.

Below right: Marcus Russell phones the future from tour bus Great White- 'We're on our way'.

CHAPTER 23

Thàinig fios dha 'san fhrois pheileir
e bhith gu spreigearra 'na dhiùlnach:
is b'e sin e Chad 's a mhair e,
ach cha b'fhada fhuair e dh'uuine.
'CURAIDHEAN' ('HEROES'), SORLEY MACLEAN

At Glastonbury, Oasis had just started playing 'Supersonic' and, suddenly, all these eggs started coming on to the stage. Everybody knows what Glastonbury can be like – the only way you can sit at the front for the last act is if you've camped there all day. If you leave, you'll never find your way back to your base. So this guy, whoever he was, must have sat there for hours and hours with loads of eggs, which missed all the members of the band anyway. How sad is that! I remember reading Noel's comment later: 'Actually, if he hates us that much, that's quite cool.'

INT. A BEDSIT, SCOTLAND – FRIDAY MORNING, 21 JULY

He pulls his inadequate bedclothes a little more tightly around his inadequate body, and stretches a pale arm from beneath his blanket defences to fish for the alarm clock. 11:00 am. A silent, unfocused, red challenge pulses back at him. He's forgotten to set the bloody thing again. So much to do. And now not even the buffer of ten stolen minutes, nah, maybe fifteen, to collate his thoughts. Eggs, good Scottish eggs. A round two dozen should do it.

* * *

INT. OASIS TOUR BUS, GLASTONBURY – MORNING.

Okaaaaay! Feeling gooooood! It's Robbo, what does 'ee want? I'm not doin' any interviews. Our Kid can 'andle 'em. Good, good, he's after Guigs. Where are we? Bus. Check the kipper. Hold on. Might be some dick behind that window. Don' wanna give it away. Sly peek. Yeah, head's still there. Good. I'm boo-oo-oo-red! Beer? Just a quick one. Whoooooah! Hold on – I'll have a line. Then a beer. Where's Bonehead? Slaphead, where is he? The dick.

'All right, Liam?'

Naaah. Robbo: graft and interviews. Naaaaah! But I'm bored – so maybe?

'No, Noel's got a couple to do. He's in with Jo Whiley now. You can just chill.'

'It's always our Kid. Always, always. What about me?'

'Well, yeah, I can probably sort something out. Everyone wants to talk to you. I just thought you'd appreciate the break.' Boo-oo-oo-red! Talk, talk, talk! Tell 'em how it is.

'OK, Liam. Catch you later.'

INT. CORNER SHOP, SCOTLAND – LUNCHTIME.

'Just the eggs, Shuggie?'

'Aye, just the eggs, hen.'

'That'll be two pounds.'

He gathers his unborn brood and jangle-tingles back into the empty street – not even a car breaks its line. Framed either side by granite tranquillity. He turns towards the station.

'Shuggie! Is that you goan tae Glastonberry?'

'Aye, right enough.'

'Go oan an giv' us yer ticket!'

Who would have thought it, Glastonbury and Oasis. Unbelievable. He fills the time before the Edinburgh train arrives making a spot-on job of nesting the twenty-four eggs in his purple and green Eurohike rucksack.

* * *

INT. OASIS TOUR BUS, GLASTONBURY – MORNING.

Chop, chop, chop, chop, chop.

'Ouuffhh, that hits the spot. 'Ere y'are, Liam.'

Snap, crackle and pop. Sheeeeeow! Slow down, slow down, steady head, steady. I – am – the Kiddy! Now I'll do the interview. Tell 'em how it is.

'Er, that was my twenty, Liam.'

Tell 'em how it is, tell 'em how it is.

Tell 'em how it is, how it is, tell 'em how it is. Where's Robbo? Lovely boy. Now's the time for talk, talk, talk. Bored, bored, booo-oo-ooooored!

'Tah, I'm just gonna go and see what Jason's up to.'

Chop, chop. A little beer. Nice cold, ice-cold. Here's Robbo. Lovely boy.

'Hi, Liam, you look bored. Come over to the beer tent, there's someone I want you to meet.'

Robbooooo! Tour float, free beer. Glastonbury . . . hundred and fifty thousand . . . fuck! Interviews?

'No, it's Sadie Frost. She was in *The Krays* and *Dracula* . . . married to Gary Kemp for a while, you'll like her.'

Sadie, Sadie, sexy Sadie. Come on! Bad little boy just moved into the neighbourhood.

'All right, Meg?'

'Hi, Robbo. Hiya, Liam. Robbie Williams has just turned up. He's brought two cases of champagne with him, but he's really nervous of meeting Liam and Noel. Where are you two going to be? I'll bring him over.'

'The beer tent. I should think you'll find us there.'

'Cool. See ya later.'

* * *

INT. TRAIN CARRIAGE, SCOTLAND – AFTERNOON.

The twenty minutes Shuggie has had to kill at the station

IF

spent carefully laying the twenty-four cardboard-coated and fragile ellipses should mean they'll all arrive in Glastonbury healthy. There are fifteen minutes to connect at Edinburgh: long enough, though, for him to pick up a carry-out. He gently eases his cargo into a corner seat on the train and begins practising menacing looks. Not so important on this short leg, but they will need to be good to ensure free space on the long run to Birmingham. A granny checks him out: 'Puir wee lamb, wha'a squent.'

The train grumbles towards Princes Street, the Castle and Waverley. He feels the unfairness of it all; it wells through him again. It is totally against the spirit of the festival. *Definitely Maybe* is just a sordid handful of terrace anthems. Where is the vibe? The Cure on Sunday – that's Glastonbury proper. What the fuck was going on in Eavis's head? Oasis playing under the Windmill of Power, it's a mockery!

* * *

EXT. HOSPITALITY AREA, BACKSTAGE, GLASTONBURY) – AFTERNOON.

Clockery, clockery, tickory, tockery. Hours to kill. Evan, you geezer. Go on, go on. Whaahaaaaay! Robbo's covered in beer. Go on, Evan, you madhead.

'Evan, for fuck's sake, man, what was that for?'

'I'm sorry. Gaaad, Robbo, I'm real sorry. Here, lemme clean you up. It was meant for the press scum, man.'

'Yeah, yeah. I know you didn't mean it. Look, we're on soon, I'll sort it myself.'

How long now? Bored. Here's a line. Back to the bus, back to the bus, back to the back of the back of the bus. You say yes, say no, you say stop, but I say go, go, go.

'All right, Liam, fancy a toot?'

* * *

INT. TRAIN CARRIAGE, SCOTLAND – AFTERNOON.

The ticket inspector is having real problems balancing down the train. Having necked a half-bottle of Southern Comfort and three Tennants Extras already, Shuggie is not at all sure he'll make it to the toilet without betrayal from his legs. Best to wait.

* * *

INT. OASIS TOUR BUS, GLASTONBURY – EARLY EVENING.

Fgggyoohhhmmmm! That was a vicious spliff. At least me fuckin' head's slowing down a bit. Nice. Still a little bit of Charlie running round in here. How long till we're on? Fucking Jacko, what are you wearing? Geezer though. Robbie Williams, who would have thought it? Geezer! Madhead, he's all right. Where's that beer? Here comes the spliff. Thank you. Think I'll chill in the back here a while. How long till we're on?

* * *

EXT. TRAIN STATION, TEMPLE MEADS, BRISTOL –
EVENING.

Shuggie is leaving the rest of this journey to fate. He'll hitchhike
to the festival, share the vibe with some like minds. He steps out
of the station a bit unsteady and leans against the grimy walls. The
realisation of eggs crashes in; he has twenty-four terminations
with him as travelling companions. His vegan psyche reels and,
overcome by injustice and seventy per cent proof, he weeps and
steels himself for what has to be done.

'Gallagher, you are gonna get yours.'

* * *

EXT. BAND ENCLOSURE, GLASTONBURY – EVENING.

That's Jonathan King, that is. Gotta have a word. That dick gave it
to Oasis big time. Time for the Kid to give it to him.

'Oh, gosh, you're Liam Gallagher. Well, you're doing well,
aren't you? It was only an opinion. My, aren't you fierce. Have a
wonderful night tonight.'

Busy, busy, busy, drive me dizzy. Quick beer. Fuckin' hell, one
hundred and fifty thousand people! This is mad! Where's Robbo?
Where's our Kid?

* * *

EXT. WINDMILL STAGE, GLASTONBURY – 10:45 PM.

The jam, the jam. The 'Swamp Song'. Fuck, our Kid's a fucking genius! Time it, time it, time it, time it. OK, the roar is down. Now for the Kid. One second more. Robbo, dancing. Let's dummy a punch to his – hah! – he didn't expect that. He's all right. Right! Right!! . . . NOW!

'COOOOO – M – M – M – M – OOAAAAOOO – N – N – N – N – N!'

* * *

EXT. AUDIENCE ENCLOSURE, WINDMILL STAGE, GLASTONBURY – LATER.

'Gallagher, you bastards! You dirty fuckin' bastards!'

Shuggie is crying like a baby. He has spent his last five pounds on a trip, and it's not taking him where he wants to go. He pulls back his arm and draws sights on his hatred and fear.

Twenty-four Scottish eggs miss a millionaire, a billionaire, a trillionaire, a zillionaire . . . bastards . . . by miles.

Losers weepers . . . losers weepers . . . losers weepers . . . losers weep.

CHAPTER 24

ICONIC MEMORIES OF THE SLAIN

Clanging fights, and flaming towns, and sinking ships, and praying hands.
But they smile, they finda music centred in a doleful song... .
'THE LOTUS EATERS', TENNYSON

Rotor speed also controls ascent – the greater the speed, the greater the ascent. Furthermore, the pilot tends to keep the rotor speed constant, altering the upward motion by the position of the craft.

As in the case of fixed-wing aircraft, the density of the air affects the efficiency of the helicopter. The ascent increases with air density.

An airborne helicopter, hovering in windless conditions, maintains an exact balance between all forces acting upon it. Vertical and horizontal flight is achieved by altering the direction of the force vectors and by changing the plane of the spinning rotors. The tail rotor is controlled by the pilot using foot pedals which allow him to maintain or increase speed.

THAT LOOKS FINE ON PAPER, but the propositions are less convincing when confronted with a lime-green one that could not be described as low mileage. The pert beauty that Liam, Bonehead and I stepped into appeared to be a veteran of at least one operational gig. Vietnam, maybe? This was our transport to Slane Castle, just outside Dublin. Oasis had played a supporting role on a number of European shows to the American darlings of college radio, REM. At Slane, we were part of their supergroup soup for the last time. It was an eventful day. The choppers were a gas, although Bonehead had to be practically crowbarred into ours. Liam lapped up every second of the ten-minute transfer from Dublin. I swear if that boy gets the money, he'll buy one, probably two, and, in a classic Liam scam, pilot both into each other at a great height and walk away unscathed.

The weather on the day of the gig was decent enough and, as we sycamored out of the sky, sliding in at forty-five, the stage and maybe the first fifty thousand odd fans or so were clearly and wonderfully visible to us. Our pilot changed down into second gear, or whatever the hell it is they do, and mirror-signal-manoeuvred us to halt on thick Irish grass. We pushed open doors and crouch-skipped under the reach of the transparent death that sliced inches away from our heads. The toilets were the best mobile gunnies REM's money could rent. They were actually better decorated than the dressing rooms. Still, and again, credit where it's due, the band's rider was already in place on arrival. It consisted then of 2 cases of premium lager, 2 bottles of Jack Daniel's, 2 bottles of good red wine, 200 Benson & Hedges and some other bollocks that you couldn't drink or smoke and, consequently, was never touched.

We'd been kicking our heels around for a few hours when a celebrated son of St Patrick entered our dressing room: Adam Clayton. He had come to wish the guys well, and convey an apology from Bono and wife, Ali, because they were not able to attend. It was a Saturday and they were out foxhunting – kidding, only kidding, of course they weren't. Adam stayed for, oooh, 90 seconds and brazenly helped himself to 40 of the band's 200 fags before buggering off. This proved, beyond doubt, the first law of celebrity introductions mentioned earlier.

There were some other bands on the bill before Oasis, all worthy. Naturally, Oasis didn't watch one minute of one set. Noel bimbled out front and had a Bacardi and Coke with his main, big brother Bod and a couple of cousins from the extended Gallagher clan. And feine sturrdy fellers they wair, now. A couple of brick shithouses on their day off. They were huge! Liam stayed backstage and got into an argument with everyone. Bonehead, Guigs and Alan killed time in a professional fashion, whatever I mean by that. Johnny Depp – a porcelain little doll with amazing cheekbones and a silly hat, but nice – dropped by to say 'Wa'ssup?' Whatever he meant by that.

Oasis did their live show. They were very good. I had to take them off stage once because the front four rows were killing themselves again. Liam made a more effective job of bringing cool than Jagger did at Altamont in 1969, but these were schoolgirls and not the San Bernadino Chapter, so no surprise there. Michael Stipe and Peter Buck from REM didn't miss a trick from Oasis' set. They were anchored, stage left and right. I had collected a full set of Oasis CDs from the band's office for Peter Buck and, when I gave them to him after the show, his response was nervous, but interesting.

'Man, I think that's the best I've seen them.' This was nice of Peter. 'With our not having played live for a while, a tough act to follow.' This was true.

'Yeah, well, it's a good job you're good.' I laid the same line on him that I had laid on Noel.

'Mmmm – thanks for the CDs, man.' Pete didn't look convinced as he slipped away.

REM were incredibly good that night and, from my viewpoint at the side of the stage, Peter Buck conspicuously worked his nuts off!

After the bands were through blowing minds, I had to go and pick up Mrs Gallagher and cousins. Brother Bod was already firing down the free drinks backstage. Finding the Gallaghers among 100,000 bodies, all moving in the opposite direction to me, was not easy. I finally uncovered them when Mrs G gave me a good dig in the spine: 'Ah, now, Robbo, thair you are. Will we go and see the boys?'

Getting backstage involved passing Slane Castle itself, a single tower that looks as if it wants nothing better than to listen to the slow advance of lichen and vine, to surrender to nature and generally call it a day. Still, it will certainly look better in a hundred years than you or I.

When I eventually brought the assorted family members together, Liam was occupied with matters of blood. He and big brother, Bod, were kicking the skin off each other.

Mrs Gallagher took one look. 'That is enough of that, now,' she announced at a level and in a tone that was as much a part of them as Liam's anger and Bod's ridiculous trousers. 'Liam Gallagher, Paul Gallagher, will you stop that!' And they did.

I wish Mrs Gallagher could have come on the road with us.

Because we stayed to watch REM, the roads out of Slane were jammed. Because the roads were jammed, we waited for a police escort. Because the police were late, the beer ran out. Because the beer ran out, the wait for the police seemed never-ending. Because the wait seemed never-ending, Liam lost his rag. Because Liam lost his rag, Noel rowed with Liam. Because Noel rowed with Liam, Liam rowed with Bonchead. Because Bonehead rowed back, Liam smashed Bonehead about the head. Because Liam smashed Bonehead, Noel's day was ruined. It should have been a great day. Because Noel's day was ruined, Liam tried to throw himself through the bus window. Because Liam tried to throw himself through the bus window, I had to restrain him. Because Liam and I were, again, in opposite corners, Noel's day was ruined. It should have been a great day.

CHAPTER 25

DIALOGUES

SCENE 4

DRAMATIS PERSONAE

MARK COYLE: Record producer and Oasis sound engineer. Long-time aid and close friend of the Gallagher brothers.

IAIN ROBERTSON: Tour manager and security co-ordinator.

WHAT'S THE STORY?

THE STAGE IS IN DARKNESS. A steady thrum of an industrial vehicle is heard. The stage lights fade up slowly, revealing the luxurious front lounge of a long distance tour bus. Sofas sweep down either side. Built into the sofa, stage right, is an elaborate console. The console features a TV screen, hi fidelity equipment, computer games and a VCR. White noise plays across the TV. The Rolling Stones' double long-playing cassette, Exile On Main Street, *beats from the tape deck. Damp traces of cocaine litter the Formica surface of a centre table. Empty beer tubes lie discarded carelessly on the floor. A shapeless mound of clothing dominates one corner. Two figures,* MARK COYLE *and* IAIN ROBERTSON, *occupy the sofas. They are in deep conversation.*

MARK: Something is very definitely not right.

IAIN: What do you mean?

MARK: Well, this should be fun. We shouldn't be having arguments at this stage in the tour over monitors. We should have our own.

IAIN: (*Sighing.*) Yeah ... would have saved a shitload of grief today.

MARK: Yeah, but, Robbo ... that shouldn't have happened.

IAIN: I know.

MARK: Liam shouldn't be expected to put up with such shit. It should never have happened. This is Oasis, for fuck's sake...

IAIN: This band always haemorrhages money on the road ... and you can't just throw money at everything.

[MARK *pulls on a beer and absently toys with a cigarette*]

MARK: We need a production manager.

IAIN: Someone with a bit of track under his belt.

MARK: You've got Marcus's ear, and Alec's, and the band's . . . it's up to you.

IAIN: Been there already. When we go back on the road after Japan, there will be a PM . . . that's a promise.

MARK: Might be too late for me.

IAIN: (*Confused.*) What do you mean?

MARK: Something is definitely not right. Not any more. I think I've had enough.

[*The conversation ends abruptly.* IAIN *and* MARK *turn their heads to the window. The lights cut to darkness. We hear the steady thrum of an industrial vehicle*]

CHAPTER 26

DIALOGUES

SCENE 5

DRAMATIS PERSONAE

MARCUS RUSSELL: Manager of Oasis.

IAIN ROBERTSON: Tour manager and security co-ordinator.

WAITRESS

OUTSIDE AN URBAN COFFEE SHOP. Unoccupied wrought-iron tables and chairs are carelessly arranged on a dirty pavement. Harsh sunlight. In the window, primary-coloured cardboard advertises miscellaneous lunch items. It is lunch-time. Business inside is brisk. MARCUS RUSSELL and IAIN ROBERTSON enter stage left, IAIN carrying some newspapers. They decide to seat themselves outside. They spend a few moments choosing the least grubby table. A young WAITRESS, casually dressed, is upon them immediately.

WAITRESS: (*Clipped friendly.*) What can I get you?
IAIN: Marcus?
MARCUS: Cappuccino, please.
IAIN: Same for me.

[*The WAITRESS scribbles the order and retreats inside*]

IAIN: Nice girl.
MARCUS: Yes.

[MARCUS *and* IAIN *lightly browse through the newspapers*]

MARCUS: (*Looking at the newspaper.*) I wonder if I shouldn't just take the band off the road altogether.

[*The WAITRESS returns with two over-filled cappuccinos*]

WAITRESS: Two cappuccinos.

IAIN: Thanks.

MARCUS: These look good.

[*The* WAITRESS *moves flirtatiously to meet a cycle courier's order*]

MARCUS: Nice girl.

IAIN: Yes.

MARCUS: (*Pensive.*) Yes, perhaps I should take them off...

IAIN: (*Stretching out his legs.*) Look, there's a chance for them to rest right now . . . and then two weeks in Japan. That's two drug-free weeks.

MARCUS: True.

IAIN: I bet you'll have a whole new band when they come back . . . no Charlie for a fortnight.

MARCUS: It's ridiculous, Robbo. I've got a sold-out show in St Louis guaranteed and the local promoter doesn't want to touch it. He doesn't believe we'll turn up and play.

IAIN: Oasis are never going to be as easy as Boyzone.

[*The* WAITRESS *comes back*]

WAITRESS: You OK?

IAIN: Great, thanks.

MARCUS: Two weeks in Japan . . . and no drugs?

IAIN: No drugs. That's the beauty of Japan. If they can bang Paul McCartney up...

MARCUS: Two weeks, and no drugs.

MARCUS *and* IAIN *pick up their coffee cups and raise them in unison in an unspoken toast.*

IAIN / MARCUS: (*Together.*) Nice girl.

CHAPTER 27

MESSAGE FROM
THE CHIEF

As for learning to fly, a kamikaze pilot might not be the ideal instructor...
EMPIRE OF THE SUN, J G BALLARD

MARCUS CLOSES THE DOOR to the make-up room and turns to his impatient audience. Oasis, fresh from the studio floor and another video, do not feel like listening. A long day has been spent generating a new marketing tool for the suits. Surely this managerial spiel can wait? Unbeknown to him, in the next room dinner is being chopped into lines at a table still bearing traces of elevenses and lunch. What Marcus has to say had better be good.

The blow is delivered cleanly. 'Mark Coyle will not be working for the band again.' It is as plain as that.

Hardly a crowd-pleaser, but he now has them in the palm of his hand.

'Naaah. Naaaaah, I'm not having it. 'E can't leave.' There is genuine hurt in Liam's voice. 'Naah, 'e can't, 'e can't.'

Marcus raises his voice to continue. 'His ears are suffering. He's noticed his hearing's diminishing and he doesn't want to lose it altogether.'

The room is filled with a cacophony of concern and opinion. Mark Coyle, sound engineer and everybody's tag-team partner, has decided to stay at home, to leave the band to tackle Japan and whatever else is coming on their own. Coyle is the man who co-produced *Definitely Maybe* and who has mixed every live show Oasis have ever performed hitherto. He is the grumpy, short-sighted and much loved 'uncle' to the whole band and he has decided he has had enough.

'He can't leave.' The voice is unanimous.

Marcus is already turning to other things. 'He can, and he has.'

* * *

It really wouldn't matter who was enlisted to fill Coyle's shoes, there was no way a warm reception was going to be in the offing. No bunting was hung and no Polynesian dancers stood in line to festoon orchids on the new boy as he checked into the Marriott Hotel in Swiss Cottage. The tour was just twenty-four hours away and Robbie McGrath was about to get a first taste of Liam – in at the deep end. Despite McGrath's superb credentials, dues paid on a long and winding road, the Coyle was considered by Oasis to be irreplaceable. Liam was determined to make sure that this fact wasn't forgotten.

* * *

Robbie, a substantial Irishman, is feeling good-natured as he extends his hand to Liam in a gesture of friendship. 'Hi, I'm Robbie. I'm the new engineer for Japan...'

'Don't give a fuck who you are . . . you won't be here in a week. I don't want to know your name.' Liam's response is more pain than anger. The cards are being marked and Coyle is casting a long shadow.

The rest of the band recognise how difficult this trip is going to be and give more gracious accounts of themselves. Although the mood is somewhat less than celebratory as we board the long-haul to Tokyo, memories of the band's last visit are enough to ensure an eagerness to get back for another dose of Oasismania. A budgetary decision has been made to consign everyone to cheap seats, including all band members – not that there are any cheap seats from London to Tokyo. Oasis carry the torch of solidarity; as there are not sufficient funds to fly twelve people business class, nobody will fly business class. Conversely, if Noel, Liam, Bonehead, Guigsy and Alan fly at the sharp end, then everyone flies at the sharp end – captains of industry *and* Marxists. At least we aren't working our passage to the far-out Far East.

As we board the plane, the guys look sweet and innocent, as they can when they put their minds to it. The stewardesses are lulled into a false sense of security. Our seats are at the back in the smoking area. It's not ideal, but at least we're not flying Aeroflot. This is not true of Liam's mate, Sid Cox. He has saved up his pennies, begged and borrowed sufficient folding green to get a seat (are there any seats?) on the Soviet airline's flight to Tokyo.

He's a braver man than I. We are all dreading twelve hours of hell, but Sidney has twenty-two hours ahead of him, in a wind-up flying brick fuelled by potatoes, his only in-flight entertainment provided by passengers filling their sick sacks.

The one alcoholic drink not provided free of charge in economy class, or World Traveller to use British Airways' extravagant tag, is champagne. Jack Daniel's costs no pounds, no shillings and no pence, which, in turn, means no peace for the cabin crew. We are all guilty of excess on this flight, and it manifests itself differently with each of us. Marcus, by nature the voice of measured balance, becomes amenable to the ridiculous. I happily provide the ridiculous. As we jet away from London, only vapour trails visible from below, I'm off on a flight of my own.

'Right, Marcus, listen, you'll love this. Support band for Earl's Court . . . U2!' An epiphany, and so soon.

Marcus has had a few himself and fails to see any weakness in my line of thought. 'Hmmm, yes. It would work, but would they do it?' His face furrows as he struggles to keep up with the irrational unravelling around him.

Noel, who is sitting in between us, is now sucked into the naïve strategy. 'Of course they'll do it. Bono, right . . . Bono: he'll be up for it.' At this point, his eyelids tire of holding up the single canopy of eyebrow, and his eyes vanish completely. Only the lower half of his face is now capable of expression. It is working extra hard to compensate for the top half and, even if his smile was divided ten times, each segment would contain its own Cheshire Cat grin. At times like this, a Gallagheresque opinion is never far away, usually monstrous in its arrogance and assumption. 'Take my first two albums . . . I'm up there with the Beatles, me.' Arrogant and assuming, yes, but utterly disarming.

Guigsy is five rows back and, once again, reliving the halcyon days when talent scouts from every major football team in the land were camped outside the family home, waiting for the chance to sign the promising midfield maestro. Bonehead, meanwhile, has no time for conversation. He does, however, remind us that he can drink everyone under the table and that 'drugs are for students'. It isn't that Bonehead doesn't like to converse, but rather that, in his list of priorities, the next bottle of red has the edge. Some of us, when in our cups, can sustain the power of speech through tricks of memory. Our tongues fly by wires forming remembered words and rushing them into service at more or less the right time. Perhaps not sufficient in itself to slip past steely blue-lit authority at the side of an unsteady motorway, but enough to satisfy the limited communicative requirements of equally disabled partners – in late, late, liquid debate. Bonehead does not possess this ability, nor anything approximating it. After the third vessel of wine, he leaves discourse to those who can be bothered with it.

Alan is very different to Tony McCarroll, the man he has replaced; he has an altogether more confident personality and integrates fully with the rest of the band. Right now, he is turning into a cartoon cockney and trying to compete with Noel. He's got the grin thing down, but it is a more open-eyed model and not as expansive – but, then, he's not making nearly as much money as the guv'nor. Liam, as one would expect, has as many different drunks inside as he has fingers to stir triple-strength potions – none is meditative and only a couple are friendly. Noel is the only one who will speak his mind in their scathing company, and then not with impunity.

* * *

By their own standards, Oasis' behaviour on the flight was exemplary. It was left to the band's crew to pick up a couple of yellow cards on our behalf.

That was a lovely move, Des, from the chubby young lightin' designer. 'E swerved alit 'is seat, crashed fooow a couple a' poor tackles, bursts into the pilot's cabin, and then, see that, lovely, 'e's tryin' to piss in the corner.

Ah, absolutely . . . a lulu.

I trailed routine apologies up the narrow aircraft walkway to dump them untidily at the feet of the Chief Purser.

We cleared customs at Narita Airport and bowled into a clean and airy arrivals hall: that place in all jet parks where excited relatives jostle with the presence of dour corporate chauffeurs, and crane to catch sight of their very own passenger who has carved continents to join them. It was at the airport where twenty or so disciples – hardcore Oasis fans – staked their first claims to follow in the band's footsteps. They were not to let the band out of their sight until we left on the world's friendliest airline two weeks later.

Our promoter for all seven shows in Japan was the Smash Corporation and they laid on representatives to ferry us to the hotel. The Roppongi Prince was situated in the Roppongi district, slap in the centre of clubland, Tokyo's version of Soho or Times

Square. Although, as this was Japan, everything seemed a lot more genteel, at least on the face of it. So we checked ourselves in and the carnival began.

* * *

Our first day is, sensibly, a day off. It is an opportunity to adjust to a new time zone that is ahead of our body clocks. The hotel, in its way, is a rock 'n' roll landmark; most bands visiting Tokyo for the first or second time will stay here. It doesn't look much from the outside, but inside it's a perfect playground for inventive minds.

The front doors are automated and slide open and shut, open and shut . . . you're too close to the door . . . come in, come in . . . we are greeted by two bellboys. They bow in polite acknowledgement of our presence.

- It is not subservience, simply a courtesy that all extend to all in this most structured and gracious society
- We return the compliment, cut across the polished black marble floor, away from the lifts; we'll check out the rooms later. Let's have a look at the pool
- Kidney-shaped, say, twisted kidney. Great name for a band: 'Ladies and gentlemen, Twisted Kidney.' The turquoise mass, dancing, chlorinated fun, is prevented from enveloping the surrounding diners by sheer sheets of clear glass. It is an aquarium, peopled by people. This is indoor *and* outdoor entertainment.
- The building rises around us and we're in the middle . . .

gazing at blue sky, but then aren't we always? I suggest we walk clockwise around the pool, past a patio where lunch is being served, the changing cubicles, the sauna, another patio, back to where we began. Now, the rooms

• Rising in the lift to nine, look down through more glass walls and watch the pool recede, we're almost in that sky, and still we can see the blue below, the hotel's heart. Room 924, welcome. This is the bathroom on the left, all facilities a little smaller than one is used to. To the right, a wardrobe and, in the wardrobe, a kimono. That's one present taken care of. The bed, low and squat and black-covered. Incidental table and mini-bar and that's your lot. Now excuse me, I need to shower and sleep. I'll see you in the bar later. We're all on this floor. Alan's in 925, Bonehead 926, Guigsy 927, Liam 928, and Noel is in 929: damage limitation by fearful management, I suspect. Anyway, not much, but it's home.

* * *

And it was to be our home for seven nights: the first week of our two-week enforced 'clean-up' campaign, because, as everyone knows, you can't get hard drugs in Japan. I wish someone had told Oasis that.

Sid Cox, having survived Aeroflot, was back among us. Here is a man who deserves some credit. He was with us through the UK, he was with us through Europe, and he was with us in America, always at his own expense. And now Japan, and Sid. Of course, having paid for his ticket, he didn't have a pot to piss in. But he had a plan. Sidney always had a plan. Manchester City Football Club – apart from the fact that they could be doing better (better get better) – produce a range of merchandise to bring them into your life for those moments that are not footling. Rise in the morning and prise your begrudging synapses out of their duvet with a cup of fresh ground, conveyed to you in your MCFC lovingly crafted coffee mug. Ease your way downstairs, still snug in club-sponsored dressing gown and generous-fit City pyjamas. Dressing gown off, tracksuit on, its proud heraldic brooch protects your heart. It's cold outside, so put on a rich mix of real wool and man-made fibres to warm the head, the hands, the throat – all proclaim City FC . . . City . . . City . . . City. Reach for keys to car and house, and there again a true-blue fob. Now, just before you dip your City shoes into the oncoming day, stop! Have you taken your medication?

One hundred true-blue fobs had travelled across oceans with Mr Cox, to be lined up next to the official Oasis merchandise and bashed out at a suitably inflated price, to ensure a ready supply of beer money for the entrepreneur. One hundred key rings at ten quid each, one thousand pounds.

A friend of Liam's took on the role of court jester to his mate and, having an enthusiastic interest in chemistry, also worked hard in his spare time to score. Drawn by unseen hands and guided by his own highly attuned sixth sense, he located the drug dealers on the inaugural night in town with virtually no effort involved at all.

Our high-rise 'playstation', remember, was situated in the heart of clubland and in the heart of clubland was a club, and in the club there was a bar, and at the bar there were three stools, and on the stools were three ladies, and they pushed dope. Coke, 'Ease', speed, acid, grass, they had it. And, because of that, my and Marcus's hopes were sent reeling. From the second he located the three Wyrdes, instead of providing the band with time out, the Japanese tour damn near sent us home in caskets.

It wasn't the 'band' setting unheard-of new records for bad behaviour in Japan; it was Liam. Guigsy had retreated slightly from what was becoming routine self-abuse. He had a stable relationship at home, which was no longer a borrowed room in his mother's and stepfather's house. He now had a split-level maisonette off the Finchley Road in London of his own choosing. . . and two washing machines. Alan was another with solid roots; a proper life away from the 'road' that fitted comfortably. Bonehead would always come out to play with Liam, or with anyone else who had a bat and ball. But given that he had turned his back on drugs a long time ago, it was hard for him to go the distance with those dancing through in white. Noel was rarely seen. When finished with the daily list of promotional commitments that seemed to fall only to him and his brother, Tokyo nights were spent with ever-greater urgency. Release dates for the new album *(What's the Story) Morning Glory?* were drawing near and the world's media was now packaging the band to its own taste and deciding where the stories lay. It was testament to Liam's talent for hellraising that my memories of what passed in those two weeks are now indelibly coloured by his non-stop attempts to kill us all. Despite our own quietude, we really did almost go back in caskets, and this from only watching Liam burn.

MESSAGE FROM THE CHIEF

* * *

The solitary writer looks around at his surroundings. Iain Robertson's head periscopes left to right, rubbing his sore neck against a collar that's in need of a wash. He has not moved for a long time from his place at a large octagonal table. The table is varnished. The varnish is dark. He takes a long sip from a deep mug of strong, sweet coffee and scrapes his eyes. It is tired. He is late. It is three in the morning and he really ought to get some sleep. That will not resolve his deadline problem. Deadlines and publishers and publishers and deadlines. The third deadline approaches and, no doubt, another argument. Arguments about layout, about photos, about fonts . . . and about titles. *What's the Story?* It does not say it for him. *Echoic Memories*: that's the title for this book; *that* says it. He pushes further into the blank, hostile page, waiting for the words to come. And they come, but slow. And you know, it was easier before. Maybe some music will help, but the writer knows that this is just a poor excuse to get away, an excuse to stop trying for just a minute. He gets up anyway and turns it into fifteen wasted minutes of browsing before settling for Lennon. He hits the play button and moves back towards the table. *Mind Games* kicks in and mind games kick in and, at last, an idea. He's bored of remembering drugs and drink and anger, sick of penning pain. Why not choose a different-coloured ink?

* * *

1: SHINY HAPPY PEOPLE

'Robbo, I'm hurting. My throat, man. And I'm knackered. I need some kip, badly, badly.' The explanation from Liam is not needed. The damage done speaks to me direct. He sounds as though someone has cut-razor-shaved down the inside of his throat.

'I'll fix up a bed away from the dressing room . . . give you a shout when it's ready.'

A nod of thanks and Liam disappears.

Right now, the quietest spot in the venue is either on stage or in the corridor leading to it. The corridor wins. Jerry-building a bed on the stage smacks a little too much of Brian Rix. It's tempting though; tonight, and for one night only, Liam Gallagher stars in *Who's Been Sleeping In My Bed*. On with the job, and with two empty flight-cases, four cushions and a towel for a pillow for an aching head, I fashion something rough and ready, but comfortable enough. The Marquis de Sade would probably turn his nose up at it, but rough, ready and comfortable will suit Liam to the bone. It will do.

In fact, he's delighted and, before you can say chop 'em out, is asleep. Liam's resting place, where he lies on his back, arms pulled forward on a shallow chest, appears as contemporary sculpture: St Martin's School of Art echoing Lenin or Mao in state. Six silent and serious Japanese stagehands file by, going about their business. As two of them dip their eyes to examine the sleeping figure, the audience is now part of the composition and the sculpture is complete. I am compelled to move forward and make sure Sleeping Beauty is still alive.

2: SHINY HAPPY PEOPLE

Monday, 28 August 1995. Imp Hall, 1-3-7 Shiromi, Chou-ku, Osaka. It's four o'clock in a stifling liquid afternoon and, you know it, another soundcheck . . . Liam has already jacked and another dressing room is feeling his gentle caress. But what, after all, can a poor boy do?

The rest of the band put their best feet forward, shoulders to the wheel, look before they stitch nine and leap into a first run-through of 'Round Are Way'. Me? I'm trying to make sense of the messages McGrath is sending at me. 'So, what you're saying, Robbie, is that, if you can work out which frequency interference patterns to run, Liam's monitors will at least sound to him as if they're working properly.'

'No,' he replies, 'you haven't got it at all. But if you can get him back up there, there's a couple of things I can try.'

That's good enough for me. I take a deep breath and go to discuss sound, science and related stuff with Liam. 'Why not give it one try, Liam? Robbie reckons there may well be a way...'

'Aaaah, Robbo, it'll be the same shit, man.' Liam is far from convinced, but follows me anyway. He scowls to the stage and is back at the mic, ignoring Noel ignoring him.

I head back to the mixing desk. 'All right, Mr McGrath, he's all yours.'

Robbie leans into his own microphone. 'Liam, thanks for giving this a go. Could you just give me a verse of something?'

'Suck my dick.'

McGrath turns to me. 'I was thinking of something more along the lines of "Supersonic".'

3: SHINY HAPPY PEOPLE

The General Manager of the Roppongi Prince Hotel has just about had it. For the third morning in a row, he has had to relocate breakfast. No choice. In a land where decorum is religion, it would be unthinkable for his valued guests to have to witness this. Will this band ever go to bed?

There is no sympathy for the weary salaryman: it's just a little fun after all; and what's a swimming pool for if not for that? So let's raise the stakes and see who's still up for it. The sinuous brunette is first; she's been pinned to Liam all night. Now she shows her hand . . . and her legs . . . her bottom . . . and her shapely breasts. As clothes slide off, she slips into the turquoise water. Liam laughs and that is the sign. There is another brunette, a blonde and a redhead and, in a flash, there are four heaps of discarded clothing and four naked females. The hotel's guardian now feels obliged to act.

Liam's own baggy, baggy, baggy shorts are off and he hurtles towards the other exotic fish and somersaults into the wet. Splish, splash, and he's taking a bath. Now Bonehead's in, now Jason, now Sid, now one and all.

Suddenly, the unsynchronised naked swimmers are surrounded by immaculate uniforms. Policemen have arrived to answer the call, to save the day, to save the manager's face. The only trouble is that naked western lithe sex is a rare treat here and the plod would rather take in the show than shut it down. The uniforms stand back and watch.

The General Manager of the Roppongi Prince Hotel has just about had it.

4: SHINY HAPPY PEOPLE

Sidney Cox is adding insult to injury. Having finished in the pool and packed, he has picked himself up and, ready to leave, is now slumped in an uneasy chair in the hotel's lobby. There are two problems: the General Manager has overcome years – centuries – of reserve and is trying to persuade the tired party animal to take his hook and sling it; Sid is so bombed he really doesn't care a whole lot. Sid's next appointment is with Aeroflot and that's hours away, so he is going to sit right where he is. Sadly, sadly, and badly, badly, he is wearing the same strides he wore last night – the ones he ripped somewhere along a twisted line. He's ripped them right around the crotch; has lost his underwear too. Now the first thing one is forced to check before he is checked in is Sidney Cox's crown jewels – schwing!

5: SHINY HAPPY PEOPLE

Bonehead has started his day with a major error of judgement. Then again, this is consistent – that's how he finished yesterday.

The Bone has laid down a challenge. None of us can believe it but, nonetheless, this time he's really excelled himself. His opponent? The band's monitor engineer, known to everyone as Jacko. The weapon of choice? Sake. The battleground? The bullet train that runs from Tokyo to Osaka this afternoon.

Let me tell you something about Jacko. Challenging Jacko to a drinking contest is like choosing the biggest sonofabitch samurai warrior in town and pulling his ponytail – there's no easy way out.

Still, Bonehead is an honourable man: he has made the challenge; it has been accepted; it will go ahead. I'm wondering when I should contact his next of kin.

We're on the bullet train. It's racing across Japan, joining the dots for us between the two cities. We're at bottle one, and the fun has just begun.

Through the window, the novelty of green Japan has worn off. We've all sipped a little sake and we're drifting in and out, kind of aware of the ongoing contest. They're at bottle four, they can take a little more – well, Jacko can.

'Can I get you a drink, Robbo?' It's Jacko, bright as a button, bringing me back from wherever I had drifted out to.

'No, thank you, Jacko, I'm fine.'

I watch Jacko deliberately walk away from me in the direction of the restaurant carnage. The door closes behind him, leaving the familiar silence, typical of the first-class engineering of the soft-upholstered first-class carriage. Gradually, I become aware of an irregular but steady intrusion: bump . . . bump . . . bump, bump . . . bump. I turn my head.

Bonehead bobs face-down, his head bouncing off the toughened plastic fold-down drinks tray that hangs from the seat in front of him: bump . . . bump, bump . . . bump . . . bumpety bump.

6: SHINY HAPPY PEOPLE

Message to Mr Robertson, Room 924.
From Mr Chief, Room 929.

Dear Robbo,
When you return could you let everyone
know the address of the club that Kondi
has arranged or yer fuckin' fired.
Yours sympathetically,
The Chief.

7: SHINY HAPPY PEOPLE

We go home, we goin' home. Noel, he gone already. Half an hour into our return to a return bout with British Airways and we are in the VIP lounge at Narita Airport. For Noel, the E he took earlier is kicking in big time – I'm on my way, I'm making it.

We are six. Lion, Pole, Stone, Alan and Nile, and me. Noel is happy tripping; G&T&E talking, but not to us. He sees sex coming in through the Can-I-See-Your-Boarding-Pass zone. We see an elegant businesswoman striding into the lounge. He sees business sex in cool grey linen and line of stocking. So why not introduce himself? ''Fare, 'e'are, oi, oi, 'e'are, 'e'are, get your tits out.' As loud as I've ever heard Nile say anything.

Lion turns to me with eyebrows raised. 'He . . . is fucking out of it.'

Lion tut tuts, and I think, irony. And can we, please, go home now?

CHAPTER 28

I DIDN'T COME TO FOOL YOU

The only thing that is unbearable is that nothing is unbearable.
RIMBAUD

THE SIDE OF MY HEAD FEELS like I need a new one. I reflect that they weren't bad punches, accurate, certainly. A pointless thought process. There are decisions to be made. Should I follow the limousine, or return to the hotel and see what the morning brings? I wave down a taxi; enough is enough for one night. *'Hotel du Nord, s'il vous plaît.'*

The heavy spring of the hotel door pulls it closed, efficiently, behind me. My bed is covered in paper, reams of documentation relating to Oasis' press schedule. I sweep all of it from the bed, crash down in its place, pick up the phone, dial Marcus and get a machine.

'Marcus, it's Robbo, listen, I've had a serious falling-out with Liam and he's gone too far...'

I carry on in that vein of maudlin self-pity for far too long. It's rambling, and incoherent, and fuelled by a kindergarten 'poor me' state of mind. Come on, Robbo, get your act together. Switch on. Time to get things right or move on.

Sleep is a temporary sanctuary – an easy escape from a world going about its business – before the pre-booked alarm call breaks in. What must Marcus think of last night's pathetic phone message? I decide to call Linda first. No reply. Then Guigsy. No reply. I'm starting to feel uneasy, bordering on sick, in my stomach. I call Alan. He answers almost immediately. I'm eager for information.

'Liam came back to the bar...'

'What happened?' I try to pull his words quickly through the phone.

'...it was cool for a while...'

'Good.'

'Not good . . . he ripped into me and Guigs again . . . really fucking vicious.'

'What about?'

Alan doesn't hear me. 'I had a go back, but Guigsy was slaughtered by it. We had a few more drinks and went back to the hotel.'

'What happened?'

'I sat up with him . . . he was shaking he was so upset, Robbo. He said he didn't want anything more to do with the band. I know how he feels; I don't wanna be in America, stuck on a bus, with that nutter.'

'Where did Liam go?'

Alan is still hurting. 'He fucked off with Linda . . . what's the matter with him? Why's he have to bite our heads off all the time? Can't he just enjoy it?'

I'm starting to get the picture. 'Where did they go?'

'Went to his room, I think.'

'For a chat, I suppose?' Great, just great. Well, now I know Linda's way of trying to diffuse the situation. She had told me again and again how much we were a team, working together, one voice pulling for the band as a whole – yeah, c'mon, team; this mess only spewed up because I was trying to defend her from Liam's spite; she obviously knows where her table's laid. More self-pity – this is getting me nowhere. I need to speak with her. 'Listen, Alan, I don't know how much of the day we can salvage. Stay in your room and, as soon as I know the plot, I'll let you know.' Alan's cool, a sane voice in all of this.

I'm up, I'm dressed, I'm ready to go. I try Linda again. No reply. I call Liam.

'Yes...' The unmistakable voice of the frontman comes back at me from a night of excess – fractured and fried.

'Liam, it's...' The line is killed; I feel the receiver crashing down. Things come and go. There's a rap on my door. I leave my phone sulking on the cabinet, its tone disconnected and dull. I open the door. It's Linda.

'Can I come in?'

As she enters, I try to find the words I want to say. 'How're you feeling?' That's not what I want to say.

She's reading my mind and small talk isn't needed. 'I spent some time with Liam last night.' She looks at me, as if for a response. I let her tell the story. 'He just needed comforting, someone to talk to.'

'Someone to talk to?'

'Yes. He's really hurt, feels the band have let him down . . . that you've turned on him...'

'Is that really what you think I was trying to do?'

'When I'm alone with Liam, I can't help seeing things his way...'

Fucking great! So she spends some time with him . . . reassuring him that this kind of behaviour is OK! What the hell's my role supposed to be now . . . trying to keep Oasis together in the middle of Paris . . . with the lead singer not only hating my guts, but now, backed up by a record-company representative, believing that I've treated him badly? She doesn't have the answer; I don't have the answer.

The first interview is scheduled for 11:00 am. I set this back an hour and start to get Alan and Guigsy together. And for Liam? Linda has agreed to ensure he arrives and the scene for a happy reunion will be in the hotel bar at midday, high noon for some sorry journalist. And for me.

* * *

It was another strange day. Alan and I were first into the room and I remember thinking its bordello colours seemed muted, the Wild West joke no longer very funny. We ordered a late breakfast of strong tea, croissants and plenty of orange juice to try to replenish our shot systems. We sat in the kind of silence usually reserved for dentists' waiting rooms. What conversation passed was stilted, the ball definitely in Liam's court. Guigsy had decided to map out his own day and had made it clear that he would not be doing any interviews with anybody, and would I kindly book his early passage home, alone.

* * *

At twelve precisely, Liam makes an entrance. He sits heavily, tosses his cigarettes carelessly on to the round table that separates us, and smiles. A lot can hide behind a smile: Jack Nicholson in *The Shining* – enough said.

Liam breaks the silence. 'Potty little night, that.'

'There's some breakfast coming.' I offer the mundane, needing to feel out where he wants to take this.

He pulls out a cigarette, puts the flame of a match to it, inhales lightly and blows out a whistle of smoke from an expressionless face. 'My fucking coat's ripped.'

So, we're playing poker. 'I'll fix it.'

'Fucking right you will.' He takes another drag and leaves the conversation there, hanging on the morning, explanations and apologies neither offered nor sought.

* * *

Unbelievably, the interviews came and went. Liam and Alan dutifully closed ranks and worked their way through the usual litany of irrelevances. However, something of a more serious nature was waiting for me: getting Guigsy on to the Eurostar and back to Waterloo.

* * *

I meet Guigsy in the hotel lobby. He has chosen not to say goodbye to anyone and so we push out into the wind and rain with no further ado. He wears an oversized navy coat bought from Burberry at its January sale. The collar is turned up in defiance of the weather, Guigsy almost lost inside – Reginald Perrin meets James Dean. We reach the station and make our way to the departure lounge. I'm stopped at the ticket check, beyond which non-travellers cannot pass.

Guigsy turns as he puts his ticket back in his coat pocket. 'I'm off then.'

I shake his hand. 'I have to ask . . . after last night, are you still with the band?'

He thinks for a second. 'I don't know, Robbo . . . I honestly don't know. Probably, yeah.'

'Well, see you, Guigsy.'

'Yeah, see you, Robbo.'

* * *

But I didn't *see* him . . . not again . . . ever.

The original plan had been to have another night in Paris and return home the next day. It seemed wiser to leave as soon as possible.

* * *

My journey home, also on the Eurostar with Liam and Alan, and not forgetting Linda, is unremarkable and still nothing is said regarding the previous night. Waiting for us at Waterloo are long, shiny cars, a reflection of the band's rising sun. Four in all: one for Guigsy; one for Alan; one for me; and one for Liam and Linda (who is still practising her own peculiar notions of teamwork). But, hang on, Guigsy should have been long gone six hours ago. Yet here is his driver standing frustrated in a prominent position, holding a card with 'Mr McGuigan' marker-penned across it. I'm later to learn that Guigsy dodged his driver on arrival, choosing to escape unnoticed. It is 7 September 1995 and tomorrow rehearsals will begin for the next leg of the Oasis tour. The shows have already sold out months in advance. That Guigsy has chosen the night before kick-off to go walkabout does not bode well. Right now, I need some time out and, going separate ways to Alan, Liam and Linda, jump into my car and head back home to the Cotswolds. I'll worry tomorrow whether I still have a job or not.

I had originally planned with Marcus to commute to the rehearsals at the Brixton Academy and decide to stick to this plan when I wake up. I arrange to collect a hire car and then later call Marcus to ensure that everything is running according to plan. It isn't; far from it. 'Hi, Marcus, it's Robbo. How's everything?'

'Robbo, I honestly don't think there's any point in your travelling up today.'

'There isn't?' My surprise is not that convincing. 'You know Guigsy went missing yesterday...'

'I thought it would be jumping the gun to call it "missing".'

'Well, he hasn't turned up for rehearsal.'

'He could be running late...'

'We've tried to locate him all morning, but can't find him anywhere.' I detect that he isn't giving me the full account of what's going down in my absence.

'Has anyone checked his home?'

'I went and personally hammered on his door . . . useless.' I let the conversation run in the hope that what has been left unsaid will be said. Marcus sounds at his wit's end. 'I've got thousands of pounds' worth of equipment and crew standing around doing bugger all.'

'Anything I can do?'

Marcus is silent for a bit and I sense that there is bad news waiting on the end of the line. 'Listen, Robbo...'

'I'm listening.'

'Robbo, there's a storm brewing and, to be frank, it doesn't look all that good for you. Are you still there?'

'I'm listening.' At least now we're getting to the guts of the thing.

'You know what went down in Paris . . . and I know what went down in Paris . . . but Liam's pissing in Noel's ear and Noel seems to be buying it.'

'I see.'

'Look, Noel's got the last word in this band . . . why don't you call him at home and see if he'll listen? I've got to go . . . try to sort this mess out. Keep your head down and we'll talk soon. Sorry I can't give you any more than that.'

I am soon to learn that there is pressure on Liam about his behaviour in Paris towards Guigsy. There is no way Liam is going to take responsibility, so the finger swings to the most obvious scapegoat: Iain Robertson, maniacal masher of lead singers. Liam's position is that I lost my head and attacked him in the street, deliberately trying to cause him bodily harm. In a phone call to Noel that night, I discover that Noel has looked more deeply into the circumstances surrounding Guigsy's absence and has discussed it with Alan. He is now no longer quite as convinced of his brother's version of events. However, blood is thicker than water and I know I'm tap-dancing on eggshells.

'Liam says that he won't work with you again.' Noel is deadpan in his delivery.

'If I'd really wanted to hurt him, he'd have come home in a box.' Noel is silent. 'You know what I mean.'

'Robbo, I really don't want to lose you . . . I've always thought you're someone I can trust . . . and there's already too many new faces around us that I don't recognise...'

'Thanks.' I appreciate his feelings, but know that there's no way around this one.

'...But what can I do? He's my brother and I'm chained to the little fucker.'

* * *

I slumped into a chair and idly picked between the bones of what had just passed. Idleness turned with the hours to a mild obsession with subtext and the night was full with the echoes of a dream that had played itself out – for me, anyway. There were to be further discussions down the line, but I'm bright enough to realise when something has become unworkable. I decided against further face-saving exercises and phoned Noel one more time. I wanted to tell him first that I would seek employment elsewhere. I didn't kid myself that I wouldn't have been pushed anyway.

I loved Oasis, loved seeing the wonder, loved sharing it all . . . being a part. Once, in a hotel room in Tokyo, Bonehead called me the sixth member of the band. Liam was there and he didn't disagree. We were all smashed, but I buzzed off hearing that, anyway. They were and are a great rock 'n' roll band and I got to walk a mile in their shoes. Do I regret not being there to the end? Wouldn't you?

Stories come back to me through the grapevine that I'm still tenuously a part of: stories of continued alarming substance abuse, of cancelled gigs and violence; stories of world domination to come; mass adulation; shifting 'units' by the container-load, the financial future assured. Who could deny they've earned it, all of it. But what concerns me still, and might concern you, should you care, is this: the next time you see them triumphant in performance, arms raised aloft to receive the favours of the faithful, are they waving . . . or drowning?

EPILOGUE

HOW DID IT FEEL to sit back and watch this truly amazing band move on and move up, realising ambitions nursed through the hard early days? Liam had once told me of how they would huddle around his mam's kitchen table, making hot, sweet cups of tea . . . and plans. Plans to prove their cynical, shortsighted and sarcastic school teachers wrong. Plans for a bigger, better, brighter future. I had a ticket, but the bus went without me.

At the height of the war for the Falkland Islands, I was on forty-eight hours standby to go. Good friends were there already. Some were dead, or dying . . . or worse, as far as we were concerned, maimed. I had a brief R&R (rest and recuperation) period, which is the way of things in the military once they decide that they are prepared to allow for your being killed: you are sent home to kiss loved ones goodbye and get a beer inside you one last time.

Standing in a sweating club – surrounded by 'civilians' laughing, drinking . . . enjoying – television screens flickered, providing a backdrop of random soundless images. Electric wallpaper pasted across club culture. One flash from the matrix caught my eye: soldiers were being 'casevaced' from a smouldering ship. The red beret, or maroon machine as we knew it, was clearly in evidence in this living hell. The images juxtaposed with my shallow surroundings brought tears of silent rage to my eyes. I could not continue to watch and left the nightclub burning with shame – a shame that is as impossible to rationalise today as it was then.

I fully appreciate that the canvas rock 'n' roll paints itself on should in no way be compared with the horrific brand of reality that is war but, in some respects, a year on the road with a band as real and committed as Oasis is like war. It's us and them; I was 'us' and now I'm 'them'. Now, when an Oasis song is played on the radio, or their image appears on the virtual jukeboxes of music television, the sensation of shame is the same and I cannot stand to listen or see – channels are changed. I feel shame that I couldn't hold it together better; that I wasn't, in whatever way, adequate to the job.

> *Experience was of no ethical value. It was merely the name men gave to their mistakes.*
> THE PICTURE OF DORIAN GRAY, OSCAR WILDE

ACKNOWLEDGEMENTS

SONG LYRICS

Prelims, p. xii   *The End*
Words and music by John Lennon and
Paul McCartney
© Copyright 1969 Northern Songs. Used by
permission of Music Sales Ltd. All Rights
Reserved. International Copyright Secured.

Chap 15,
p. 156, 157   *Floorshow*
Colour picture   Words and music by Craig Adams, Gary Marx
section caption,   and Andrew Eldritch
p. 5   © Copyright 1982 Gary Marx/BMG Music
Publishing Ltd, 69–79 Fulham High Street,
London SW6 / Eldritch Boulevard Ltd,
administered by Polygram Music Publishing

Ltd, 47 British Grove, London W4. Used by
kind permission of Music Sales Ltd. All Rights
Reserved. International Copyright Secured.

Chap 15, p. 160   *The Supermen*
Words and music by David Bowie
© Reproduced by permission of EMI Music
Publishing Ltd, London WC2H OEA.
© Reproduced by permission of Chrysalis
Music Ltd, London W10 6SP.

Chap 15, p. 161   *Bennie and the Jets*
Words and music by Elton John and
Bernie Taupin
© Copyright 1973 Dick James Music Ltd,
47 British Grove, London W4. Used by kind
permission of Music Sales Ltd. All Rights
Reserved. International Copyright Secured.

ACKNOWLEDGEMENTS

PUBLICATIONS

Chap 3, p. 29   Yeats, W B, THE SECOND COMING in
Collected Poems of W B Yeats, (London:
Macmillan, 1950)
Reproduced by kind permission of A P Watt
Ltd on behalf of Michael Yeats

Chap 3, p. 33   PLANETARIUM, by Michael Lutin, in *Vanity
Fair*, May 1994.

Chap 3, p. 41   PLANETARIUM, by Michael Lutin, in *Vanity
Fair*, May 1994.

Chap 4, p. 48   Aleister Crowley: DIARY OF A DRUG FIEND
(York Beach, ME: Samuel Weisner, 1995)
Cover material used by permission.

Chap 6, p. 65   Soyinka, Wole, MADMEN AND
SPECIALISTS, Methuen, 1993. Reprinted by
permission of Reed Consumer Books.

Chap 14, p. 143   Plath, S, MIRROR, in Hughes T (ed.),
Collected Poems, London, Faber and Faber
Ltd.

Chap 15, p. 160   Huxley, Aldous, THE DOORS OF
PERCEPTION, London, Chatto & Windus,

1954. Reproduced by kind permission of Mrs Laura Huxley.

Chap 16, p. 169   2 lines (p.129) from THE COMPLETE ODES AND EPODES by Horace, translated by W G Sheperd, 1983. Reproduced by permission of Penguin Books Ltd.

Chap 23, p. 233   Maclean, S, CURAIDHEAN, IN REOTHAIRT IS CONTRAIGH: TAGHADH DE DHAIN 1932–1972 (Spring Tide and Neap Tide: Selected Poems 1932–1972), bilingual edition, Canongate Books Ltd, Edinburgh, 1988.

Chap 27, p. 261   Ballard, J G, EMPIRE OF THE SUN, Victor Gollancz Ltd, 1994.

PUBLICATIONS (WITHIN PUBLIC DOMAIN)

Chap 2, p. 15   More, Henry, CONJECTURA CABBALISTICA, London, 1653.

Chap 4, p. 48   Aleister Crowley, DIARY OF A DRUG FIEND, W Collins & Sons, London, 1922.

Chap 4, p. 51/52   From de Cieza de Leon, Pedro, THE SEVENTEEN YEARS' TRAVELS OF PEDRO DE CIEZA DE LEON THROUGH THE

ACKNOWLEDGEMENTS

MIGHTY KINGDOM OF PERU, 1532–50.
Extract from Martingdale, Coca, Cocaine,
and its Salts, London, 1886.

Chap 4, p. 53   Shakespeare, W, ANTONY AND CLEOPATRA,
London, J & R Tonson, 1758.

Chap 6, p. 71/72 Boyce, S S, HEMP (Cannabis sativa),
New York, Orange Judd Company, 1900.

Chap 7, p. 77   Shakespeare, W, THE TEMPEST, London, 1725.

Chap 9, p. 93   Joyce, J, ULYSSES, London, Egoist Press, 1922.

Chap 10, p. 109 Byron, Lord, THE DESTRUCTION OF
SENNACHERIB, in Murison W Bums, Byron
and Campbell's Shorter Poems, London,
Percival & Co, 1893.

Chap 11, p. 115 Ovidius, Naso, METAMORPHOSES, London,
William Blackwood and Sons, 1871.

Chap 12, p. 126 Martingdale, W, COCA, COCAINE AND ITS
SALTS, London, H K Lewis, 1886.

Chap 13, p. 135 Kant, I, CRITIQUE OF JUDGEMENT, in
Kant's Critique of Aesthetic Judgement,
Oxford, 1911.

Chap 17, p. 179   Stein, Gertrude, THE GEOGRAPHICAL
                  HISTORY OF AMERICA, or the Relation of
                  Human Nature to the Human Mind, USA,
                  Random House, 1936.

Chap 17, p. 188, Debries, Dr E, HOLLYWOOD AS IT REALLY
189, 190, 191   IS in Seen by the Camera, London, George
                  Routledge & Sons Ltd, 1932.

Chap 19, p. 207   Willies, N, Lowheel, J, Griswold, R, THE
                  WORKS OF EDGAR ALLEN POE, New York,
                  J S Redfield, 1850.

Chap 21, p. 219   Carroll, L, THROUGH THE LOOKING
                  GLASS AND WHAT ALICE FOUND THERE,
                  London, Macmillan and Co, 1893.

Chap 24, p. 243   Tennyson, Lord Alfred, THE LOTUS EATERS,
                  London, Gay and Bird, 1901.

Chap 29, p. 288   Wilde, Oscar, THE PICTURE OF DORIAIN
                  GRAY, London, Collins, 1931.